A History & Celebration of

The Playhouse Theatre

Weston-super-Mare

Best wishes
Sam
x

Samantha Ball

 *redcliffe*

First published in 2019 by Redcliffe Press Ltd.,
81g Pembroke Road, Bristol BS8 3EA

info@redcliffepress.co.uk
www.redcliffepress.co.uk
Follow us on Twitter @RedcliffePress

Text © Samantha Ball
All images courtesy of *Weston Mercury* unless otherwise indicated

ISBN 978-1-911408-57-4
British Library Cataloguing-in-Publication Data
A catalogue record for this book is available from the British Library

Design and typesetting by Stephen Morris www.stephen-morris.co.uk
Minion pro 10.5/13

Front cover: Montage of photographs included in the book
Back cover: The Playhouse stage. Photograph courtesy of Vicki Gray

Printed and bound by Short Run Press Ltd, Exeter

Redcliffe Press Ltd is committed to being an environmentally friendly publisher.
This book is made from Forest Stewardship Council® certified paper.

FSC
www.fsc.org
MIX
Paper from
responsible sources
FSC® C014540

Contents

Introduction

It's hard to imagine when sitting in the auditorium of The Playhouse Theatre waiting for a show to start that you're seated exactly where food produce such as bread, fish and fresh meat was once sold. Equally hard to imagine is that if the rebuild of the theatre hadn't been approved after having been destroyed by fire in 1964, the site could have been turned into a car park instead.

Although I have had the privilege of performing at The Playhouse, I feel my place is more in the audience and, as an audience member, I have lost count of the number of performances I have watched at the theatre over the years. With musicals being my favourite form of theatre, I have enjoyed watching 'Dreamboats & Petticoats', 'Blood Brothers', 'Save the Last Dance for Me' and 'Priscilla Queen of the Desert', but I have also enjoyed many other forms of entertainment, including comedians, ballets, tribute acts and plays.

In 2016 I was lucky enough to start working in the box office at the theatre on a casual basis (alongside my full-time job in the NHS), taking bookings both over the phone and in person, as well as handing out tickets before performances and dealing with everyday queries about the theatre. I feel lucky to be able to say I work in the theatre as my enthusiasm has never dampened and I enjoy helping others experience the love of theatre. I share with Mark Thompson, General Manager, the enjoyment of watching the audience arrive for a show and seeing the excitement for the performance ahead.

With many star performers having graced the stage, The Playhouse has a rich history, but there have also been many times in the past when the theatre has been threatened with possible closures. It also may not have been rebuilt if members of the local council had been listened to due to the amount of money it was predicted to take to re-build it.

The Playhouse holds a charm of providing locals and holiday-makers in the seaside town of Weston-super-Mare with an enjoyable theatre experience, and while other theatres may prefer to put on week-long shows, The Playhouse combines this with one-night-only acts, giving people the opportunity to experience different genres of theatre in a short space of time.

The Playhouse has developed over the years to reach out to as many people and generations as it can, and will always strive to do so as Weston's home of entertainment. Boasting a capacity of 664 seats, the theatre has hosted a variety of shows throughout its history, including the ever-popular pantomime, which has attracted a host of household names to spend their Christmas in Weston.

September 2019 will mark the 50th anniversary since The Playhouse theatre re-opened its doors following the devastating fire, and it was with this in mind that I decided to do some research into the history of the theatre: to find out how it came to be and what kind of entertainment it had provided before the fire and in the 50 years since.

With such well-known names as Sir Ken Dodd, Frankie Howerd and Cilla Black as well as Michael McIntyre, Kevin Bridges and Jane McDonald having trod the boards at the theatre, The Playhouse has a rich history of attracting performers and shows no sign of slowing down.

But before we start looking to the future, let's go back to when the theatre was first established.

Old Market Hall.
Photograph courtesy of The Friends' Open Day, from Andrew Gibson.

The Creation of The Playhouse

Weston-super-Mare's High Street is the town's oldest road, and from 1825, where The Playhouse now takes pride of place, was situated an open-air produce market, 'The Market Hall', built by well-known local builder Mr Charles Addicott, providing poultry, butter, bread and fish. In what would be a shock to people nowadays, livestock was also slaughtered on the site to provide fresh meat to customers. It has been mentioned that at the entrance to the market there was the fruit and flower stall of Mr Fred Wall, and towards the back was a second-hand bookshop owned by Mr Grace.

In 1899 architect Hans Price gave the building a new design, making it into a covered market hall, and in 1946, as the market was no longer being used, the decision was made to convert the building into a temporary concert hall with seating all on one floor.

Plans for converting the High Street market hall into a theatre were announced in the local press, and details were shared in the *Weston Mercury & Somersetshire Herald* on 6th April 1946.

> Within the limitations, no effort has been spared to ensure a cosy little pre-fab theatre. It will seat 460 people and the box office will be approached by a foyer which will have cloakrooms on either side. The walls of the auditorium will be adorned with murals painted by members of staff from the local council – down one side will be a countryside scene and a vista overlooking the sea will be on the other.
> The stage will be 31ft 9in wide and 23ft deep with a proscenium opening of 24ft with a height of 17ft. The stage will be 4ft higher than the auditorium floor and beneath it there will be a band room and two dressing rooms. Dressing rooms for principals will be provided on either side of the stage and exits will run underneath them.

Washbasins and other facilities will be fitted and a sunken orchestra pit is also included in the plans. However, with the proposed adaptations, it is not possible to include heating.

A big problem is the height of the building, but to temporarily overcome this, hessian drapery will be used in the form of a tent which will dip down on either side of the murals.

When resources permit, the rear of the building will be built to allow the 'flying' of scenery.

Since the council's intentions to convert the market hall have been announced, offers to put on performances have been received by many sources with some of the most famous personalities in the concert and revue worlds interested.

A total of £15,000 was spent on this conversion – including £3,000 paid out in war reparations for the loss of the Grove Park Pavilion (a glass-roofed bandstand used for summer entertainment) during World War Two – which included removing the last of the shops alongside the market but leaving four flats on the high street. However, despite the building saying goodbye to its market days, during wet weather the unheated auditorium was still prone to the smells of livestock.

This theatre was named 'The Playhouse' and became a rival to the Knightstone Pavilion (later known as the Knightstone Theatre), which had opened in Weston in 1902.

The Opening of The Playhouse

The Playhouse Theatre opened its doors in 1946 and to this day is still a well-loved landmark of Weston. While originally it could only seat 500 people, directors at the Knightstone Theatre feared it could potentially take their business and viewed it as a real threat.

The first show to be performed at the theatre, on Saturday 15th June 1946, was the comedic 'Frivolities', produced by Hedley Claxton and featuring performers such as Dickie Hassett and Arthur Turton. This 'carnival of wit and humour' was performed over the summer season and, according to the 'World of Entertainment' section of the *Weston Mercury & Somersetshire Herald*, provided a 'marvellous mixture of ballet, comedy and song'.

Excerpts from the show were broadcast on BBC radio in August 1947 and the house was so full that the commentator Nicholas Crocker had to be crammed into a corner of the stage. The broadcast was a fine boost to Weston entertainment and put The Playhouse Theatre firmly on the map. The show went up against 'Summer Rhapsody' at the Knightstone Theatre and while many would have thought that one would win out against the other, critics commented that not many resorts had the advantage of two top-quality shows.

Following the comedy, the Weston Concert Orchestra made its first appearance on Sunday 8th September directed by Lemeul Kinsey with an event titled 'On Wings of Song' and featured the welcome return of the popular baritone, Charles Dorning.

However, following the successful opening season, criticisms were raised by members of the public as the Weston Council Chamber announced plans to close the theatre during the winter months, but the theatre announced in

October 1946 that the winter season would be repertory, with the Avon Players presenting 'Without the Prince' by Philip King.

To prepare for the winter season, it was decided that heating would be installed in an attempt to make the theatre more comfortable (and to try to get rid of the livestock smell!). This installation took place in October 1946, and was achieved with the introduction of 18 novel gas heaters which were placed overhead, with thermostat controls to ensure even temperatures throughout the auditorium.

The Early Years

At the beginning of 1947 the Borough Council Entertainments Committee faced criticism for its autumn/winter season policy at The Playhouse, and was accused of making a 'bold move' as the theatre moved from repertory to variety, as variety was seen as costly. Afternoon concerts that had taken place at the theatre were discontinued and moved back to the Winter Gardens (another local entertainment venue) to take place on Sunday afternoons.

However, the year started off well with a season of twice-nightly variety shows presented by Will Hammer Theatrical Enterprises which, in addition to running variety at a chain of theatres, was associated with pantomime and film production.

'A well-balanced show', which it was hoped would set the standard for future bills, provided something for everyone. Its first week included burlesque acrobatic dancers, singing, dancing and comedy, with the standard remaining consistently high throughout its run, and it didn't stop there. With different acts taking to the stage each week, variety was definitely the way to describe the show, with subsequent acts including Maurice Fogel, the amazing mind reader and a South African wizard, fire-eater and sword swallower!

It was noted in the *Weston Mercury & Somersetshire Herald* in February of that year that variety was big news and, although the Borough Council was concerned with the takings of the theatre, it was acknowledged that the atmosphere was warm and audiences were very appreciative of the 'amazingly cheap entertainment' being provided during the winter. The idea to use the theatre during this time was hailed as 'different, bright and clever'.

Yet, despite this success, there was drama at the Weston-super-Mare Council Chamber on 17th February when members of the council keenly debated the winter policy. The Entertainments Committee felt that the theatre should be closed for the winter months, as figures showed substantial losses, but thankfully the majority decision was that opening was justified. One councillor raised that The Playhouse should be operated in summer only and could be hired out at other times to local societies or am-dram companies for non-profit purposes. Pantomime had also been considered over the Christmas period, but this idea was scrapped in favour of continuing with variety.

In April it was revealed that Hedley Claxton's 'Frivolities' would again occupy The Playhouse stage in the summer and, judging by the success of its debut the previous year, it was expected to be first rate. But before that, ex-wartime troop entertainer Bunny Baron – the 'rare-bit' – topped the bill at the theatre in May, wearing blazers that were as 'colourful and overpowering as his personality'. Sharing the stage with Roy Walker, Britain's youngest debonair who combined dancing and vocals, the two of them kept up the high standard of performances the locals had come to know and love before handing over to 'Frivolities'.

Once again Dickie Hassett was the principal comedian during the season, and the variety was kept up, with the show changing every Wednesday and Saturday to keep it fresh for audiences and encourage twice-weekly visits.

As the theatre kept audiences entertained, thoughts were turning again to the winter policy, in a bid to decide whether or not to keep the theatre open. The Playhouse was regarded as a temporary building which in winter was at a disadvantage, since people couldn't be lured away from the cinema or the stars they could hear on the wireless unless a famous star was on the bill, but unfortunately the theatre was viewed as not being able to book famous names as it didn't have the 'capacity' to take big money.

In August the decision was made to allow Will Hammer Theatrical Enterprises to take over The Playhouse from September and to run shows for a year. Variety would be the key, and the theatre was confident that, given the continuity over the previous 12 months, it would be possible to make a success of variety. There would be no play season, and for eight weeks during the winter amateur productions would be held. It was also decided that variety would follow the next summer with another resident company.

*

Will Hammer's season opened on 22nd September 1947 and included talent competitions which contestants could apply for at the stage door up to 30 minutes before the show, so no one knew what kind of show would take place! The supporting cast for this week included, among others, 'Six feet of fun' comedian Tommy Cooper, followed by the sunshine personality of Benny Hill.

Following a successful summer season, it was commented that the variety being provided by the theatre over the autumn wasn't receiving the support it deserved – a theme which has been repeated on and off throughout the years. However, following the professional shows, it was now time for the amateurs to take over and from 9th to 13th December, The Alexandra Players performed 'See How They Run' by Philip King, a show later reviewed as a 'laughter tonic' and the 'most amusing show Weston amateurs have given in a long while'. This success was followed by the Weston Junior Arts Club, who presented an adaptation of 'The Water Babies' under the direction of Miss Joyce Tidman.

*

February 1948 saw Weston's second annual Drama Festival take place featuring amateur groups from as far as Wales, and throughout the week the festival drew good attendances. In a show of support, when The Red Triangle Players took over The Playhouse for their turn, they found a message chalked on the mirror from the previous group, saying 'Good luck'.

However, despite the success of the Drama Festival, which was won by Bristol WEA (Workers Educational Association) Players, it was announced in March that although the shows throughout the winter had been first class, the winter variety experiment had failed, with the theatre making a loss of £4,500. In a bid to help, the Weston-super-Mare Society of Arts offered to take the theatre off the hands of the council for the winter months and run it as an arts centre, but this was declined.

Brighter times followed when the summer saw 'Holiday Highlights' presented by Will Hammer and Michel Kebby become the resident show,

Poster advertising 'Holiday Highlights', 1948.
Poster from Playhouse Archives. Author's photograph.

providing indoor sunshine to full houses come rain or shine, with the programme changing every week. The show opened to packed audiences, boosting the finances of the theatre with Councillor Cooper, Chairman of the Entertainments Committee, calling it 'the best show we have ever had at The Playhouse'.

Variety gave way to drama in October, with the Somerset Original Play Festival taking over, which was followed by the theatre's very first pantomime 'Babes in the Wood' on 27th December. It was noted that this was a 'balanced miniature Christmas show, but could have had more in it for adults'.

*

During the early years, The Playhouse was considered as the theatre for repertory, with the Knightstone Theatre being for professional shows, but despite this, The Playhouse provided a mixture of entertainment and in 1949, following the first pantomime, celebrity concerts and drama festivals were intermingled with performances by amateur societies. One such celebrity concert was held on Wednesday 19th January by Weston-super-Mare's Society of Arts, starring soprano Joan Cross, tenor William Herbert and pianist Ivor Newton, all of whom were of international repute and provided a sell-out show.

In February, while the Knightstone Theatre continued to stage its pantomime, 'Jack and the Beanstalk', The Alexandra Players provided comedy at The Playhouse in the form of Noel Coward's 'Private Lives', which was followed by the Somerset County Drama Festival and the third annual Weston-super-Mare Drama Festival.

March of that year saw the Entertainments Committee accept an offer from Mr H.A.E. Smith, Vice Chairman of the Hotels Association, to provide and promote a Playhouse 'cabaret show' to be held between 12th May and 4th June, as well as another offer from Hammer Productions Ltd to put on a full summer show. Mr Smith stressed that 'Intimate Cabaret' was not an amateur production and he was working on providing a full professional bill. He was quoted in the *Weston Mercury & Somersetshire Herald* as saying: 'I'm not expecting to make a penny out of it, but I am providing the cabaret to simply provide some entertainment for our visitors'. As the show opened, it was acknowledged that there were points which could do with smoothing out, but the show was something different in the difficult season of the year.

'Holiday Highlights' returned in July with the appreciation of audiences noted and it was commented that if this was anything to go by, the theatre would have a successful season. But, although audiences remained a fair size, the heatwave didn't do it any favours, as indoor entertainment lost some of its appeal for the public during the hot weather.

Discussions about the use of the theatre during the winter months remained ongoing throughout the year and the winter policy came under attack again when the recommendation not to operate during the winter months was brought up for discussion at the Borough Council meeting. During the previous meeting it had been recommended that the theatre could be put out for hire at £60 a week, with staff provided by the council, as closing the theatre was the only way to invite private offers for short periods of time. The previous policy had lost the theatre £1,000 during the winter, as although the bills were excellent, there were no stars of note performing so people turned to the radio or cinema for entertainment instead.

After a two-week run of 'Sunshine Pierrots' headlined by George 'Snowey' Ford, a production which had transferred to the theatre from another Weston entertainment hall, the Cove Pavilion, on 19th September, it was announced that The Playhouse would be closed except for casual bookings, in accordance with the council's decision. This wasn't a popular decision; however, audiences did support the shows that appeared, which included The Alexandra Players performing 'The Sacred Flame', a personal appearance by celebrated hypnotist David Wolfe, and a Christmas attraction 'The Beggar Prince', which was described as a 'fairy play with music'.

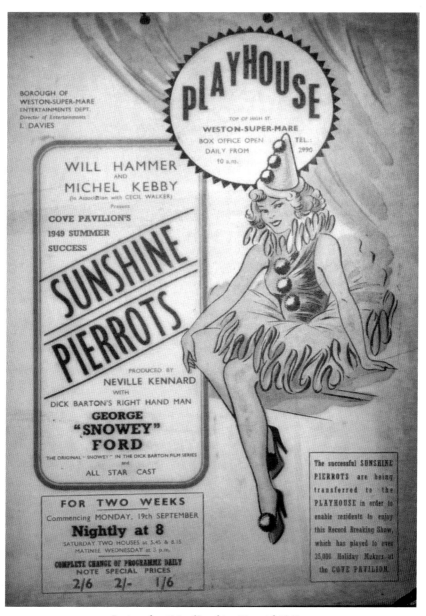

Poster advertising 'Sunshine Pierrots', 1949.
Poster from Playhouse Archives. Author's photograph.

The 1950s

The start of the 1950s was quiet at The Playhouse, with the first performance, an absorbing mystery called 'Duet for Two Hands' by The Alexandra Players, not scheduled to take place until 11th February 1950. It was noted that the entertainments programme for the town had reached a new winter low as, following the end of the panto run at the Knightstone Theatre, the Winter Gardens Pavilion, the Knightstone Theatre and The Playhouse were all closed, with the choice of entertainment limited to dances at the Kings Hall or films at the three cinemas.

In March it was announced that, following the final of the Somerset County Drama Festival at The Playhouse, which was held on 24th and 25th March, there would be an extended repertory season in the summer performed by a company made up from The Rapier Players of Bristol Little Theatre. The idea came from Will Hammer and Michel Kebby and it was hoped that as the season had been extended from 10th July until 30th September, the company would present many of the outstanding successes they had performed at the Little Theatre during the past year to a new audience.

However, over the Easter period bad weather meant that indoor entertainment was relied upon more than ever, and The Playhouse didn't disappoint. Audiences described The Alexandra Players' performance of 'Pygmalion' as 'first rate' and 'in no way amateurish', thanks to the hard work of the cast under the direction of Joyce Tidman, who had a brilliant record of work in the town.

Before the summer season began in June, audiences were kept entertained at the theatre by a variety of amateur performances, including the fourth annual Weston-super-Mare Drama Festival (which was criticised by the Mayor for not having local support from either societies or audiences), the

Junior Arts Club's presentation of 'Robin Hood' and the Junior Arts Festival, which attracted a record entry of almost 500 participants from as far and wide as Bristol and Bridgwater.

'Your Family Favourites', a concert party including comedy sketches from Scottish comedian Dave Walker as well as dancing and musical items, opened the summer season on 19th June for one week, prior to The Rapier Players opening their repertory season in July with 'Quiet Weekend' by Esther McCracken. Praise was high for this production, with comments made describing it as 'a brilliant debut, a really brilliant performance' which 'produced the most satisfying evening'. It was hoped that the fortunes of The Playhouse would be transformed by this season, as although previous experiments to boost finances as well as audiences had been unsuccessful, this one was proving the opposite.

A ballot was opened in August to find out whether there would be sufficient support for extending the repertory season for The Rapier Players at the theatre, with at least 1,500 names needed for the experiment to succeed, and in September it was announced that although only 1,164 people had voted in favour, the season would be extended for 'as long as they received adequate support'. Councillor D.H. Miller-Barstow, Chairman of the Entertainments Committee, said: 'It is entirely up to the public, if they support the players then they will stay, if not then they go.'

While support for the extended season was encouraging at the start, audiences started to dwindle as the season entered October, with one performance being attended by only 150 people. The experiment became subject to week-to-week review, and the weeks became vital in the bid to decide whether all-year-round drama could be supported at the theatre. However, it was announced in early November that unfortunately support had declined to such a point that the experiment had failed and the council's contract with The Rapier Players would expire on 25th November. Many people who had attended the theatre during the repertory season expressed their disappointment as The Rapier Players had gained many supporters during their stay and had maintained repertory of a high standard at the theatre. Director of the company Ronald Russell also expressed his disappointment, saying:

It is most disappointing ... before we decided to try a winter season over 1,000 people promised their regular support, but only about 25% of the audiences were coming every other week. About 500 actually took up their tickets and about 100 said they would support the theatre when they could. We were told that to hold Weston audiences they would need to do more serious plays, but 'Arms and the Man' was the worst supported of the lot!

It was commented that only a few more patrons would have made the difference in keeping the season going, but Ronald Russell said it was more likely that 500 more patrons each week would have been needed.

Despite the audiences for The Rapier Players waning over the season and the experiment being a costly one, the Entertainments Committee suggested that they should be invited back the following summer, with Michel Kebby, Managing Director of Will Hammer Theatrical Enterprises, saying: 'As a resident of Weston-super-Mare, I do feel we are making a mistake letting a first-class company leave town merely because of slightly reduced attendances'. Ironically, at the end of the 20 weeks of repertory the company had provided at The Playhouse, the audience for their final performance, a comedy called 'The Patsy', was practically full, ending a successful season, after which the theatre closed until March 1951.

*

The use of The Playhouse at the beginning of the following year was sparse, with an Easter attraction called 'Bonaventure' from The Alexandra Players in March followed by a local play called 'Beside the Severn Sea', which was performed by a cast drawn from all the amateur dramatic societies in Weston to mark the Festival of Britain. The play was written about events which happened in the town during Queen Victoria's Golden Jubilee in 1887 and attracted a good audience. However, the town's enthusiasm for drama had decreased so much that the Weston-super-Mare annual drama festival, which had been previously held at the theatre, was discontinued due to the lack of participation from local societies.

The Rapier Players returned for their second season at the theatre in June 1951, with most of the plays they put on being comedies, and it was clear from their opening performance that the high standards they had set the previous year were to be continued.

While all of their performances attracted the support of the locals as well as holiday-makers, one play staged in September 1952, 'A Murder has been Arranged', for which The Rapier Players had changed the setting to a local area, got the audience questioning whether the company was aware of how close they were performing to a real-life murder scene, as in 1840 a local pub landlord had been hanged in Taunton for the murder of his wife just yards away from where The Playhouse now stood.

When The Rapier Players ended their season at the theatre, it became home to another company, The Unicorn Players, who transferred from the Knight-stone Theatre as it neared its panto season. It was announced that if they proved successful, they would stay on at The Playhouse until the end of February, and despite a slow start with one performance drawing in an audience of only 50 people, the company slowly gained support.

As the repertory season continued at the theatre, interspersed by local performances by The Alexandra Players and charity performances, audiences were getting used to a high standard. Keen to continue that tradition, a new company presented by Will Hammer and Michel Kebby called 'The Playhouse Repertory Players' took up residence at the theatre in the summer of 1953; one member was Bernard Cribbens, who later became known as 'Perks' in the popular family film 'The Railway Children'.

No professional companies expressed interest in using The Playhouse during the winter months, so it was acknowledged that any use over this period would be by local organisations. It was agreed that the Weston Society of Arts would make use of the theatre during certain dates in January, February and March, and a special rate of £28 for a period of four days would be charged.

Discussions were held by the Trading Undertakings Committee about proposals for the theatre in the coming year, but when at the end of 1953 there didn't appear to be any bookings until the summer season in the following July, there were suggestions that the council could invite tenders to install a projector and run a cine-news theatre. However, this idea didn't take off.

*

With The Rapier Players' return to the theatre for another season in the summer of 1954 complaints were raised, during the annual meeting of the Society of Arts in May, about the look and feel of The Playhouse, despite the theatre having housed a number of performances since its opening. The outgoing Mayor of Weston-super-Mare, Alderman D.H. Miller-Barstow, promised that the complaints would receive the attention of the Borough Council and that improvements would be kept in mind.

Comments noted at the time included: 'I think The Playhouse looks dreadful for visitors. It obviously appears what it is – an old market place turned into a theatre.' It was agreed that the theatre could be made more comfortable, with a member of the meeting saying: 'If you strip back the hessian and put in a false roof, I think the council would get their money back in next to no time because it would make it more cosy and comfortable.' It was also stated that while the overhead heating was a good idea, a lot of the heat was being lost through the hessian. The hessian also proved difficult to work with in times of rain, as one performer had had the indignity of being dripped on during a performance due to rain building up on the drapes. The duckboards were also commented on, with it acknowledged that many people tripped on them on their way to their seats, and Councillor Mrs Battiscombe said that ladies who wear high heels would prefer rubber strips.

Following this discussion, the Weston-super-Mare Trading Undertakings Committee proposed improvements at the theatre and approved a scheme estimated to cost £2,000 for a permanent plasterboard ceiling (the next year a fibreglass roof was installed for a fraction of the price). They also considered a scheme to increase the seating capacity by 100, which would mean taking up a portion of the arcade, but this was later dismissed as the income couldn't justify the expense.

The Chairman of The Alexandra Players, Mr Frank H. Beech, also spoke out about the facilities of the theatre in a letter which appeared in the *Weston Mercury & Somersetshire Herald*, agreeing that they 'leave much to be desired'. However, the following year the company wrote another letter, but this time thanking Mr B.H. Flavell, General Manager of the Catering & Entertain-

THE PLAYHOUSE

Mr. Frank H. Beech, chairman, The Alexandra Players, writes:

"The members of this Society were pleased to read 'Everyman's' recent criticism of the Playhouse, and we would like to take this opportunity of saying how fully we agree with his statement.

"The lighting is totally inadequate and completely outmoded. There are no 'spots' on stage, and this is the basis of all normal lighting in contemporary theatre

"We suggest that the Council invite a recognised expert, such as Mr Brenner, of the Bristol Old Vic, to advise on equipping the stage economically and effectively. Behind stage, too, the general facilities for casts leave much to be desired.

"Thank you, 'Everyman,' for bringing this matter to public notice."

Mr Frank H. Beech's letter in the *Weston Mercury & Somersetshire Herald.*

ments Committee, following the improvements that had been made to the theatre. Praising the changes, the letter stated:

> The much needed extra lighting, the condition and maintenance of the dressing rooms and co-operation of the resident staff, made the mounting of a production a much less arduous task than it has been in the past. It is very encouraging to think The Playhouse is on the way to becoming at last a 'real theatre'.

*

Another bid to establish winter variety at the theatre was trialled in early 1955 by Will Hammer and Michel Kebby. While it was shorter than previous attempts – consisting of just two Saturday performances – it failed, with the draw of the cinema on a Saturday night as well as the television proving too much competition. However, the theatre was used by amateur societies until the welcome return of The Rapier Players in the summer. But when their season ended in October it was announced that, although they had maintained consistently high standards of repertory theatre throughout their years of performances, due to lack of support, the summer season – like the winter season – could unfortunately no longer continue. The great summer weather had inevitably caused a drop in takings, but it was felt that a different form of entertainment should be trialled during the next summer with the hope expressed that repertory could make a welcome return in the future.

*

Variety was the choice of entertainment for the summer of 1956 and while Hedley Claxton presented entertainment at the Cove Pavilion as well as 'Gaytime' at The Playhouse, television was blamed for the dwindling audiences throughout the season, although it did attract a full audience for its final weekend.

The following summer, however, The Playhouse returned to a season of repertory, with Peter Haddon's The Famous Players taking up residence and, in a show of support, their season was extended until September with one theatre-goer presented with free tickets for her commitment to the theatre. Mrs F. James was given two free tickets by Mr A.A. Bryant, Box Office Manager, when she became the 2,500th person to enter the theatre that season. Having not missed a play during their run, she commented that The Famous Players 'are a really good lot of troupers'.

By the end of the 1950s, The Playhouse was in need of more improvements following those that had been made in 1954, and it was decided that a scheme to improve the theatre both inside and out must cost no more than £5,000. It was agreed that every effort should be made to increase the revenue of the theatre, as well as generally upgrading the facilities for patrons and visiting companies, and by mid-June 1959, The Playhouse had been

Poster advertising a run of plays by The Famous Players, summer 1958.
Poster from Playhouse Archives. Author's photograph.

given the comfort and ambience it deserved, with it now being considered a 'first-rate little theatre'.

Changes under the £5,000 improvement scheme included the auditorium floor being revamped with the removal of the duckboards to prevent audience members tripping up, as well as a slight re-arrangement of the seating to allow clear visibility of the stage from every seat along with more conventional lighting. The box office was moved and the foyer was extended out to the pavement to include a cloakroom for patrons – this was achieved by purchasing the former greengrocer's shop, which used to be on the corner of the street. The overhead gas heaters were replaced by radiators on the wall, and the walls were given a more contemporary design. These improvements transformed the theatre into one which could become more popular with the town all year round, and this proved fruitful when it was announced that the theatre would be open during the week after Christmas.

However, despite the improvements to the auditorium and front of house, the dressing rooms were described as 'appalling', with Councillor H.S. Allen saying he was surprised that artists used the backstage area of the theatre: 'I know someone will say that others are worse, but that does not mean that we should have a pigsty. I think for the benefit and dignity of this town, we ought to make this a nice comfortable theatre.'

It was noted that local people were very dependent on the theatre and, with amateur societies keen to book throughout the winter, further changes should be made to ensure its ongoing use, and therefore another improvement scheme was launched. A list was put together following consultation with both professional and amateur companies who had used the theatre, as well as drawing on the experience of staff members and this included an improved backstage area, previously described as 'primitive' and 'shocking'; more stage lighting; new toilet facilities; additional wing space and possibly more dressing rooms than the 'two and a bit' the theatre currently held. It was recommended that the changes be completed as soon as possible and that revenue should be used before a loan was applied for.

Amateur societies The Wayfarers, The Red Triangle Players, Weston Dramatic Society, The College Players, The Crown Players and The Oldmixon Players put a rota together for the autumn and spring so they could all get their fair share of use of the improved theatre before the professionals took over in the summer. The first amateur performance to be held in the improved theatre was 'One Wild Oat' by Weston Dramatic Society in October 1959.

Unfortunately, though, with new facilities at the theatre such as the ability to fly scenery, and with more space and extra full-time staff, the theatre became more expensive to hire, and over the years, one by one, amateur societies have had to drop out of using it.

The 1960s

As the theatre entered the 1960s, it was announced that, thanks to their previous success, The Famous Players' summer season would start earlier than before and guest stars would make appearances during the season. The first of these was to be well-known TV star Richard Murdoch, followed by popular stage and TV comedian Claude Hilbert, who starred with his wife Enid Trevor in 'The Chiltern Hundreds'. The introduction of guest stars brought plays to the theatre that might not necessarily have otherwise appeared, as each guest star chose the play they would appear in, and audiences were grateful for this. It was acknowledged at the end of the season that the experiment had been worthwhile and had kept the company on its toes.

Following on from this success, the company was listed as 'one of the best 50 permanent repertory companies in Britain' in a national magazine and it was recommended that they returned to The Playhouse the next summer, which they did. Peter Haddon, actor and manager of the company, was quoted as saying 'The limitations of your Playhouse stage would naturally prevent any elaborate productions, but by concentrating on quality and from time to time augmenting the company with well-known leading players of national reputation, I have little doubt that I should be able to maintain a high standard of production', and the players did just that, with 'full house' signs placed outside the theatre throughout their next summer season at The Playhouse.

However, The Famous Players' summer season came to an abrupt end in September 1962 following the sudden death of Peter Haddon, after which they said they could no longer perform in Weston as every effort had to be put towards keeping their headquarters at Wimbledon Theatre open. The company were praised for staging 13 plays during their final season, with 92 different actors taking part and for their productions over the years, which had been seen by over 25,000 people.

But while The Famous Players had enjoyed three successful seasons at the theatre, we mustn't forget the amateur societies who were also gracing the stage. With The Red Triangle Players, Weston Dramatic Society, The College Players and The Wayfarers all taking turns to provide comedy and drama to supportive audiences throughout the years, Weston Operatic Society made their first appearance at the theatre in November 1961, when they performed 'The Mikado'. Their experiment to bring a musical to The Playhouse stage proved very satisfactory as nearly 3,000 people attended and raised money for both St Margaret's Home (a holiday home for disabled children) and the British Empire Cancer Campaign.

A mix of entertainment continued at the theatre and a rare opportunity for the town of Weston to see and hear a live opera production was given when Opera for All were booked to perform 'Marriage of Figaro' in early 1962. The opportunity proved too good to miss, with all the seats sold for the one-off performance, and support was so good that the company enquired about appearing again the following year. Returning for two nights in February 1963 by invitation of Weston Society of Arts, they performed 'The Secret Marriage' and 'La Boheme', with the standard of the young performers described as being of the highest calibre, and audiences on both evenings were very receptive.

*

Following the departure of Peter Haddon's The Famous Players, the largest repertory company in the country, Charles Vance's Group of Three, became the next company to stage a summer season at The Playhouse. They opened their 22-week season on 31st May 1963 with the record-breaking musical 'Salad Days', starring comedy actor John Inman, who went on to star in TV's 'Are You Being Served?'.

Boasting 65 actors, ten stage managers, four designers and five producers, the company – whose season was extended by two weeks due to its success – provided a mix of comedy, thrillers and drama as they entertained the town for the summer and also helped the theatre host a world premiere when they performed Dennis Spencer's newest and funniest farce, 'Always in Trouble', for a week in August.

During one week the company brought in the highest takings at the theatre for any season – a week Charles Vance was unlikely to forget as it was also the week he became a father to his daughter Jacqueline. The Borough Council's Trading Undertakings Committee added its praises to the success of the company, commenting 'We have had a wonderful summer of quality entertainment'.

As the curtain came down on The Group of Three's season at the theatre in mid-October, Charles Vance, who attended the last performance with his wife and young daughter, thanked the audience after the final curtain, saying: 'On behalf of my wife and all the members of the company, I would like to thank Weston for the way we have been received. We have had a wonderful reception both inside and out of the theatre', and that support was set to continue as it was agreed before the company left, that they would return the next year.

*

Christmas 1963 saw the first professional pantomime take place at The Playhouse Theatre following a bid by four amateur groups to stage it. Previous pantomimes in the town had been held at the Knightstone Theatre, but it was felt that The Playhouse was more central and easier for people to get to, especially following the severe weather of the previous year. So, on Christmas Eve 1963, Bunny Baron opened the 'Grand Family Panto' 'Robinson Crusoe', starring comedian Sandy Powell, starting a tradition at The Playhouse that continues to this day.

Playing to over 11,500 people during its run – including many full houses – 'Robinson Crusoe' was a big success. Commended for its colour and abundance of gaiety, it was well suited to the intimate setting of The Playhouse. Support was encouraging as patrons from surrounding areas attended the theatre by the coachload, and special party bookings were also made. Mr Val Gibbons, Deputy Entertainments Manager, said at the time, 'This is the most successful panto we've ever had', with audience participation hitting a high right from the start. Producer Bunny Baron, who was hosting his third pantomime in the town, recalled that the last time he had been on the stage at The Playhouse was in 1948, when it was more like a market hall, but even then he had had a lot of fun.

*

Now, 1964 is known as the year The Playhouse Theatre was destroyed by fire, but before this incident occurred in August, the finals of the Junior Arts Festival were held at the theatre, as well as performances by The Red Triangle Players, Weston Dramatic Society and The College Players, whose performance of 'Under the Sycamore Tree' was the last amateur performance at the theatre before the fire.

May saw the return of Charles Vance's Group of Three to The Playhouse but this time with a smaller company of 16 actors. Opening their season with 'The Marriage-Go-Round', the company enjoyed success, as before, and also welcomed newcomers such as Australian actor Norman Coburn who went on to play Donald Fisher in the Australian soap opera 'Home and Away'.

In a change from the comedies the company had been performing, it was decided that from August, the thriller 'Love from a Stranger' by Agatha Christie would be performed to keep the audience on the edge of their seats until the end of the season, but no one could have predicted the real-life thriller that was about to happen.

The greatest drama in the history of The Playhouse was yet to come.

The *Weston Mercury & Somerset Herald*, Friday 28th August 1964

The Fire

During the early hours of Saturday 22nd August 1964, a fire described in the press as 'the worst fire in Weston since the Second World War' broke out at The Playhouse Theatre, destroying everything but the front and side walls, although these walls were later demolished after being deemed unsafe. With the alarm raised simultaneously by residents and by a patrolling policeman at 1.00am, PC Herbert Poole said at the time:

> I was on duty near the GPO. I happened to look towards the theatre and saw smoke curling up. It was not a great volume, rather like a garden bonfire. I judged it to be in the Market Lane area. There was no glow or any sign of a fire, but I had got only half way across the road when the roof at the back caved in and then there was one big sheet of flame belching up. I ran to the front of the building and by that time the flames were pouring in from the main part of the building into the foyer and it seemed to be ignited all the way round.

Rousing residents in the flats above the theatre and helping them to escape, PC Poole undoubtedly helped save their lives. One of the fire-fighters who helped tackle the blaze commented that it was lucky there was no wind at the time, as it would have caused the fire to spread. The theatre quickly became a 'furnace of fiercely burning wood and molten metal', with the heat of the fire said to be so intense it made the windows of nearby properties crack.

As the fire made its way through the theatre, the need to evacuate the flats above was immediate, but Mr and Mrs Evans told how they 'just had time to dash back in to get enough clothes to look decent,' while Mr and Mrs Hornett did the same and also managed to save their budgie Sparky.

Although the flames licked around the adjoining buildings, praise was given to the 24 firefighters from Weston-super-Mare, Bridgwater and Winscombe who prevented it from spreading. An onlooker from a flat opposite the theatre, Mr Matthew Silver, told the press that he was getting prepared in case the fire did spread:

> We were watching from the start and the firemen didn't seem to be able to get to the flats at first because of the intense heat. I was frightened as I thought our building may be damaged. We shifted all our property out the way in readiness.

Karolina McIntyre has fond memories of living near the theatre and remembers the fire clearly, including the embarrassment of running to the Royal Hotel in her nightie. She recalled:

> Me and my sister used to play at the back of the theatre with other local children near the bottom of the fire exit where performers would go to smoke. If there were any props left over from a production they would give them to us – I remember playing with dolls that were left behind.

When I asked Karolina about the fire, she described the view from the skylight window in her bedroom:

> Me and my sister were in our bedroom and I remember commenting on how orange the sky was, but didn't think anything of it until the fire brigade broke our door down and told us to leave. I remember us having to run away from our flat towards the Royal Hotel and it was embarrassing as I was in my nightie.

Directly after the fire, the flat wasn't safe to live in, so Karolina and her family had to leave. When the theatre was eventually rebuilt, Karolina remembers her disappointment at the frontage, 'It was like a charcoal cover so it gave the appearance that the theatre was still burnt, but thankfully it was eventually painted over.'

Following the fire, John Moore from Sports Ltd, who had a property adjacent to the theatre, donated ten guineas to the Fire Services Benevolent Fund as

The fire in progress. Photograph courtesy of The Friends' Open Day, from Andrew Gibson.

External view after the fire.

Aftermath of the fire.

Exterior of the theatre
after the fire.

a thank you, but little did he know that in 1970 he would be saying thank you to them again!

With the flames put out and the devastation of the fire revealed, a 70-foot mobile crane was used to remove unsafe parts of the theatre walls which had warped in the heat, and 55 feet of scaffolding was erected. Large planks of wood were placed in a leaning position across the windows of the shops on the opposite side of the road, which pedestrians used as a tunnel to walk through while the area was being prepared for demolition, and barriers were put up to keep out the large crowds who gathered to see what remained of the theatre. As a result of the fire, it was discovered that the pinnacle of the theatre had moved approximately 1.5 inches from its original position.

Tenants from the flats above lost all of their possessions, as did The Group of Three Drama Company who had been using the theatre at the time to rehearse their play 'No Time for Love'. Losses at the theatre included costumes, scenery and props totalling £2,500, as well as contracts and wages, but thankfully no lives were lost. All in all, the total cost of the damage was estimated at £75,000.

Pete Magor, who has worked at The Playhouse on and off since the 1960s, recalled the aftermath of the fire: 'The company lost all of their scenery and sets. In the old days we didn't have a scene dock; it wasn't configured like it is now. There was no real storage.' A steel cabin trunk was later found intact among the remains, but the clothing inside had been reduced to ashes. Another item salvaged from the fire was Charles Vance's make-up box which he had used for 18 years, but unfortunately it was too badly damaged to be used again.

Having been informed of the fire at 2.45am, Mr Vance said: 'I haven't seen anything like it since the blitz. I came straight down and went to the back of the stage knee deep in water.' When talking about items which had been lost to the fire, he said:

> One of the things I don't normally keep in the theatre is recording equip-
> ment, but unfortunately because of special effects for the play I took it in
> here and that's gone too. There is hardly an actor in this company who has

Charles Vance's letter to Weston residents.

Charles Vance surveying the damage after the fire.

more than what he stands up in.

The cast of the drama company, who at the time included Sue Nicholls (now known as Audrey Roberts in 'Coronation Street'), were determined that, in accordance with theatrical tradition, 'the show must go on' and they were moved to temporary accommodation – the Assembly Rooms at the Town Hall – where they continued to rehearse and perform. Charles Vance was quoted as saying: 'Next week's bookings were the best of the season so far and we don't mind where we go – even if it's only in a tent!'

Pete remembers helping them relocate:

When the theatre burnt down we set up the stage and the seats for the makeshift theatre. The Stage Manager for the Company was Sue Nicholls – she used to do a lot of voice-overs and was brilliant on dialect accents. She was very nice and we related to each other, being of virtually the same age.

The Charles Vance Group of Three company advertising their season at the Assembly Rooms, 1967.

As the company had lost their sound equipment in the fire, once again Pete was on hand to help: 'I had to supply the company with the sound effects after the fire. I had quite a few in those days and that's how I got to know Sue, working alongside her.'

When the show opened at the Assembly Rooms, which had been transformed simply, but practically, into an attractive theatre, the result was a sell-out, with Weston's amateur societies showing a strong presence in the audience in a show of sympathy and support for the players. The Mayor and Mayoress also attended the performance, along with local residents and holiday-makers, with the keen sense of anticipation bringing an almost gala atmosphere to the evening. Mr Vance later wrote a letter to the town of Weston on behalf of the company to express their thanks to everyone who supported them following the fire.

Charred remains of The Playhouse.

Dampening down the remains.

The Group of Three remained performing at the Assembly Rooms Theatre for the next couple of years while The Playhouse was being rebuilt, meaning that the town of Weston didn't miss out on their performances, which had become popular with the public.

Amateur companies booked to stage productions at The Playhouse were invited to move to the Knightstone Theatre so that they would not miss out on performing, and it was agreed that although the Knightstone Theatre was larger than The Playhouse, by the courtesy of the council, costs would remain the same.

*

Inspecting the damage.

All that was left of the theatre.

The cause of The Playhouse fire has been the subject of rumours, with some saying it was due to a discarded cigarette in the stalls (as smoking was allowed inside in those days and there were ashtrays on the back of the seats, this is a plausible explanation), while others have speculated that it was due to faulty lighting above the stage. In a bid to find out the official cause of the fire, I contacted the fire brigade in the hope of finding the original report, but unfortunately they don't have records going back that far. However, Pete Magor confirmed to me that it was due to a cigarette:

> The fire brigade said it was a cigarette in row D in the stalls. It started in the auditorium and couldn't have been electrics as there weren't any in the auditorium. The old theatre was one of the last theatres to run on DC

electricity, so there may have been issues with it, but I can only go with what the fire report said.

With the town devastated by the loss of the theatre, the speed with which the council put in place emergency arrangements led to hopes that there would be an early announcement about the rebuild and that it would take place without issue. During a meeting of the Borough Council on 30th September 1964, thanks were expressed to the fire brigade, whose prompt action and skilful work in containing the fire had prevented a potentially bigger disaster, as well as to the property companies who had rehoused the residents and to contractors Wimpey & Co Ltd, who provided materials and labour to make the building as safe as possible.

Discussions were also held at that meeting about the future of The Playhouse, and while it was confirmed an insurance settlement had been approved and rebuilding the theatre was the main topic of discussion, there were also talks about relocating it. One councillor suggested the theatre be built on the site of the Winter Gardens' tennis courts, which were considered to be a 'white elephant' in the town, and which would provide visitors with car parking facilities, something they didn't (and still don't) have, while another suggestion was to build a rest centre for the elderly where the theatre had stood. Thankfully, there was no support for either of these ideas and it was eventually agreed that as no suitable alternative location could be found and the cost of relocating the theatre would add at least another £50,000 to the total cost, The Playhouse should be rebuilt on the original site.

However, it would be another five years before the theatre would open its doors again.

The Rebuild

With a cheque for £79,880 in insurance money, it was hoped that the rebuilding of The Playhouse would get under way swiftly; however, some nine months after the fire, plans for the theatre were still under discussion.

Preliminary plans for an intimate theatre of modern design by Mr Duncan Kaye, an architect from W.S. Hattrell & Partners, were submitted to the Borough Council and discussed at a special meeting of the Catering and Entertainments Committee in May 1965. Suggestions for the new theatre included increasing seating capacity to between 600 and 700 by including a balcony, although it was important for the theatre not to lose its 'little theatre characteristics'; improved facilities for both performers and audience members; and an increased stage and backstage area as well as a green room and rehearsal room. It was said that the cost would be no more than £150,000 and would be a 'sensible workable theatre without a lot of frills'. A projection room was also considered within the plans, but as it would add up to another £12,000 to the cost, this idea was dropped. It was hoped that the theatre would be ready for the 1966 season, but this would mean a great deal of extra expense and it was soon made known that it was unlikely the theatre would be ready until 1967.

Initial plans were approved in June 1965, and Mr B.H. Flavell, General Manager of the town's Catering and Entertainments Committee, told them: 'We are going to have a theatre at which we can offer a higher standard of drama than we have ever had before.' The aim was for the theatre to be an arts centre for the community, with local amateur societies already express-ing interest. But with the cost of the theatre causing concern to rate payers, and an announcement from the government in July 1966 about cuts to funding in local councils, the future of The Playhouse was in doubt – if

An architect's design for a new repertory theatre.
Photograph courtesy of The Friends' Open Day, from Andrew Gibson.

permission wasn't granted to rebuild it as a theatre, one idea put forward was for the site to be used as a temporary car park.

A further report presented to General Manager Basil Flavell and the Catering and Entertainments Committee by W.S. Hattrell & Partners on 10th December 1965, stated that they wanted to build a 'first class theatre with at least 650 seats'. Boxes were also included in the seating plan, which they anticipated would 'add to the intimate atmosphere we are aiming to provide'. They were confident that the new figure of £160,000 was economical in cost for a fully equipped theatre, and it was predicted the rebuild would take 12 months. As well as increasing the seating capacity, other improvements to the theatre included greater space between the seats to allow more leg room, a purpose-built scene dock alongside the stage (stage right), and three floors of dressing rooms. Air conditioning was also being considered for the summer months.

To cover the cost of the rebuild, which was now at £218,396 due to the expense of meeting building and fire safety regulations as well as the government selective employment tax and fees for contractors, the Borough Council applied for a loan of £141,000, the repayment costs of which were included in the increased amount. But concerns were raised that the increasing costs were too high, and questions were asked whether the town could afford it. There were also allegations of unnecessary delays in progressing the plans for the rebuild, but Basil Flavell disputed this, informing the public that 'a project to replace the theatre had been very much in the public mind and every time a decision was required or consideration needed, a special meeting was called to avoid delay'.

The Catering and Entertainments Committee recommended in November 1966 that, despite cuts to funding and increasing costs, the rebuild should go ahead, and the town put together ideas of how to fund it. However, following a local petition signed by 400 people and sent to the local government minister, a criminal investigation was demanded into increasing costs and concerns about expense. A public inquiry was scheduled to take place on 14th March 1967 to discuss the amount of money needed to carry out the agreed plans.

During the inquiry, it was stated that with the size and importance of Weston as a town, it should have a properly equipped and well-designed theatre, and unfortunately the Knightstone Theatre couldn't be adapted enough to fulfil the needs of the town. This was good news for The Playhouse, as it was also said that there would be increased costs and a considerable delay if the theatre was to be rebuilt on an alternative site. Mr Flavell stated that although 'it has been suggested in the press that a suitable theatre can be built for £100,000 more or less, perhaps it is a fact that a theatre could be built for this sum, but not one suitable to the needs of the town'.

A grant from the Arts Council of £8,000 helped towards the overall costs – and The Red Triangle Players did their bit to help by donating £25 to the scheme, with plans to donate more – but it wasn't until August 1967, three years after the fire, that building work actually started.

In a bid to extend the stage area of the theatre, two properties behind the theatre site were purchased and, following the discovery of a seam of peat under the rubble, a decision was made to build the theatre on 'piles' instead of directly on the ground, meaning there was a need for a more expensive form of superstructure to support the theatre.

*

Now that the rebuild was finally under way, the contractors faced difficulties, working on top of each other in cramped conditions in a bid to get the theatre up and running as soon as possible. As the work continued, thoughts turned to the opening performance.

While it was hoped it would go ahead in July 1969, it was suggested that a summer variety show topped by a star artist would be the best way to open the theatre, but some expressed the view that, as the theatre was originally designed for plays and amateur productions, opening it with variety wouldn't be right. A councillor on the Entertainments Committee was quoted as saying: 'We want to get full houses at The Playhouse in the first year. We want people to feel there is something worth seeing there and get into the habit of attending. We shall have a building of which we can be proud.'

In the end, a repertory performance with a star name was decided upon, with the Brian Rix Company chosen to do the honours, and an opening date of 4th July 1969 was fixed. At this time Basil Flavell also revealed his plans for future performances, departing from the idea of an amateur season and instead staging amateur performances in between other productions. His idea was to 'introduce a cross section of people to the theatre' and to 'create a new ticket market', saying 'I think The Playhouse is going to fill a demand that few people realised existed.'

Despite bad weather slowing the progress of the contractors, plans were put in place to ensure the theatre would be completed in a suitable time frame and on 25th November 1968, Peter Hess, Mayor of Weston-super-Mare, made theatrical history when he performed the ancient tradition of the 'topping out ceremony' on the roof of The Playhouse. The ceremony, which marks the completion of the roof height and is said to ward off evil spirits, was completed when the Mayor filled in a small hole on the nearly finished roof with concrete, and was presented with an ornamental trowel from the contractors for his efforts. Mayor Hess said at the time of the ceremony, referring to the completion of the theatre:

> We have waited and waited and hoped through periods of financial strain to see signs of the phoenix rising from the ashes, and today although the bird cannot yet stretch its wings, we can rejoice in the fact that it has reached its full height.

He also added: 'the theatre will become a home for the arts in Weston'.

Mayor Peter Hess completing the topping out of the theatre.

Speech at the topping-out ceremony.

Handing Over Ceremony

Although the theatre was now complete, the handing over ceremony didn't take place until Saturday 5th July 1969. During the ceremony the theatre was handed over to the new Mayor, Councillor David Driver, by Mr Enoch Linton, Area General Manager for the contractors Dudley, Coles, Long & Co Ltd. Receiving a token key, he said:

> This is the day for which we have all been waiting and it is with particular pleasure that I accept on behalf of the corporation, the key of this fine modern theatre. The Borough Council and its officers had the courage and foresight to pursue this ambitious scheme. Tonight Brian Rix and his company will bring the theatre to life, but don't let us forget that today another cast is giving its final performance – a cast comprising a great number of people intimately concerned with the building and development of the new theatre.

He was referring to the many people who had had a hand in bringing the theatre back to life.

Speeches were made at the ceremony about the many frustrations and setbacks the theatre had suffered since the fire, but it was also noted by Councillor Driver that 'The Playhouse is the first modern purpose-built theatre in Weston-super-Mare and it will play a part in the entertainment and cultural life of the town.'

Architect Duncan Kaye of Messrs W.S. Hattrell & Partners talked about the issues that had been faced in building on and working in a confined space without risking damage to the buildings either side, saying it had been a

The token key to
The Playhouse.
Author's photograph.

Plaque marking the
re-opening of the
theatre in 1969.
Author's photograph.

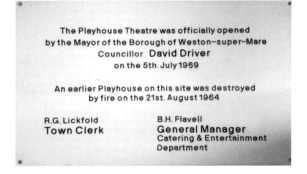

The Playhouse Theatre was officially opened
by the Mayor of the Borough of Weston-super-Mare
Councillor **David Driver**
on the 5th. July 1969

An earlier Playhouse on this site was destroyed
by fire on the 21st. August 1964

R.G. Lickfold
Town Clerk

B.H. Flavell
General Manager
Catering & Entertainment
Department

'difficult undertaking.' He also spoke about the criticism that had been made about the exterior design of the theatre saying:

> It is a very easy thing to design buildings which are pretty mediocre. I think this building has character. It looks like a theatre and I think and hope that people will come to like the exterior in time.

The decorative panels on the facade were the work of London sculptor William Mitchell, who had also completed work on Liverpool Metropolitan Cathedral of Christ the King. Talking about the auditorium, he said:

> Everyone has to be able to see and to hear. That sounds all very simple, but in fact it takes a lot of hard calculation, careful design and to some extent scientific examination of the acoustics. One important thing is to achieve a relationship between the performers and the audience and this is an extremely difficult thing to do.

Following the ceremony, a tour and inspection of the theatre took place during which it was praised as being 'one of the best, if not the best theatre in the country'. Brian Rix, who attended the luncheon which followed, expressed how he felt about being the first to perform at the theatre, 'I must say how proud and delighted I and my company are at opening this new Playhouse. It is a splendid occasion and one on which you are all to be greatly congratulated.' He then memorably said on stage at the end of the first performance, in relation to the new theatre, 'It works!'

*

When I met with David Driver and got talking about his involvement with The Playhouse through his role as former Mayor, it seemed to me as if the memories came flooding back easily, and he was able to talk about them as if they were yesterday:

> I know I was the first councillor on the scene after the fire as I lived in Cecil Road and used to walk down by the park to go to Waterloo Street and always went by The Playhouse. I saw the fire engines the morning after, which were a shock and went straight to my office to call Basil Flavell who was the councillor in charge of catering and entertainments. He had a lot of drive and enthusiasm for The Playhouse which really helped it get going.

David recalled the differences of opinion expressed after the fire:

> It really was a battle over two to three years to save the theatre. It was a question of whether both The Playhouse and Knightstone were needed, but Weston was different in those days as a lot more people used to go the theatre. There was also a row about relocating it as half the councillors wanted to move it to the promenade, but we argued whether people would want to be out there in the winter. We did battle and it was only after we got permission for the use of two shops either side that it was agreed to rebuild the theatre on the same site.

David also recalled how he watched the progress of the rebuild, saying:

I remember going into the theatre at regular intervals and saw the concrete being put in for the levels of the seats. There was no roof at one time and it was pouring with rain – I thought, how are they going to make a theatre out of this?'

Thankfully, they did, and after four years of hard work since the fire, The Playhouse was restored, with the extension taking its seating capacity from 500 to its current 664. The final cost of the rebuild totalled £230,000 – equal to just over £3 million in today's money.

Re-opening of the Theatre

Now, there are *three* dates to take into consideration when talking about the re-opening of the theatre.

'Let Sleeping Wives Lie', the first production to be held on the new stage, was booked for a ten-week season, starring Brian Rix and then Leslie Crowther, who had previously starred in the play at the Garrick Theatre in the West End. Following a special preview held on 5th July 1969 (the first date) for people who lived close by, the first performance opened to a full house on 7th July (the second date), with Brian Rix, who later became Lord Rix, calling the rebuilt theatre 'absolutely marvellous'. He later wrote in his book *Tour De Farce: A Tale of Touring Theatres and Strolling Players (from Thespis to Branagh)*:

> The Playhouse is a delightful little theatre. The backstage facilities were particularly pleasant, which showed at long last actors were being considered at the original planning stage. They were certainly good enough to attract other big names for the next two summer seasons which I presented.

Pete Magor remembered spending up to four weeks in the run-up to re-opening the theatre, putting in lights and slowly turning it from a blank canvas into a working theatre, and the 'get-in' for the production – which is when the scenery and equipment is taken into the building – was particularly stressful. This was because the extension of the theatre had decreased the lane behind it to only eight feet wide, meaning the lorry was unable to access it, so all the scenery had to be carried from the lorry, down the lane to the stage door and into the theatre before it could be assembled, whereas it would normally have been unloaded straight into the theatre from the lorry parked directly outside – not exactly a great start to the re-opening!

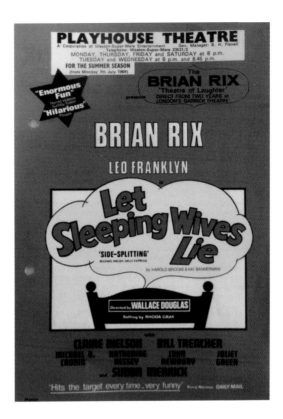

Leaflet advertising
'Let Sleeping Wives
Lie'. Playhouse
Archives. Author's
photograph.

David Driver told me that the night before the theatre opened, he, Basil Flavell and Norman Haskins, Chairman of the Catering Committee, wanted to make sure everything was ready:

> The night before it opened, Basil, Norman and I went into the theatre and we sat on every seat – every one of them between the three of us – to make certain they all had good views. I was wearing a leather jacket and the side walls of the stalls were almost like brickwork and it was all rough – that was the modern thing. I ripped my jacket on the wall and said: 'we can't have this'. Basil said 'leave it to me' and we got a lot of people out of bed – we had a couple of carpenters who got this posh wood and put it on the wall as a feature. That was the night before it opened. We then went for a drink in the bar afterwards.

Exterior of the theatre advertising 'Let Sleeping Wives Lie'.

David explained why he is aware of *two* dates in relation to the opening:

> There were so many people involved that the council hit on the idea of having
> two openings. The first was on the Saturday when the key was handed over,
> with only a small group of people present, including the architects, builders
> and the usual VIPs from the council. I remember going on stage to make a
> speech with the cast around me at the end of the performance and it lasted
> about 20 minutes as there were so many people to thank. Brian Rix then said
> his piece and, as far as the audience were concerned, that was the official
> opening. But then on the Monday we did exactly the same thing, only the
> general public were in the audience, so they were under the impression that
> they were at the official opening. That's why there are two dates. I had to do
> my speech again on the Monday and the cast had thought that on the Satur-
> day I had spoken 'off the cuff', so when I said the same things I could hear
> Leo Franklyn, who was behind me say 'it's all the same as the other night'
> and as I was talking he used his walking stick to try and distract me by
> prodding me with it!

It was reported, following the run of 'Let Sleeping Wives Lie', that the farce
had been a 'most wonderful success' with most performances playing to near
full houses and over 50% of audience members coming from surrounding
areas such as Bristol, Nailsea and Backwell, and even as far away as Taunton
and Bath. Due to this success, negotiations were already ongoing about
another Brian Rix production for the next summer.

However, despite this run, the *formal* opening of the theatre took place on
15th September 1969 (the third date) with the world premiere of a new play
called 'Wesley: A Man against his Age' which was written by Jack Emery, the
theatre's Assistant Director. Rehearsals for the show were screened in a BBC
programme, which also showed officials from the Arts Council of Great
Britain attending a performance on 19th September 1969. Despite being
designated the formal opening of the theatre, there was no opening
ceremony or speeches following the performance, so it was essentially left
to speak for itself, and it did just that when it was reported that, over the
four days of the show, 1,400 people had attended the theatre to watch. The
play brought considerable publicity to the theatre and helped bring the total

'Let Sleeping Wives Lie' in production.

audience figures since the first opening date to over 10,000.

*

With only a few vacant weeks in the diary until the end of the year, Basil Flavell reported that there were many different forms of entertainment booked for the autumn season, which it was hoped would work in favour of the theatre, saying: 'In the first place they will show the capabilities of the theatre and we hope will introduce the theatre to different sorts of audiences, although we hope of course that some patrons will go to all of them.'

The first amateur performance on the new stage came from Weston Dramatic Society, who performed Terence Rattigan's 'The Sleeping Prince' over the week commencing 13th October 1969 to rave reviews. They regarded being the first amateurs to perform on the stage as 'an honour and a privilege', and the praise for the theatre didn't stop there. Letters of appreciation were received from companies that had performed at the theatre, with the Royal Ballet describing it as 'one of the best, if not the best we have played'.

With a sell-out concert from The London Mozart Players resulting in a queue of eager patrons waiting outside in the hope of returned tickets, the total income for the year at that point was nearly £3,000 over the target figure, which no doubt pleased the Entertainments Committee.

1969 was brought to a close with the grand family pantomime 'The Sleeping Beauty', starring Derek Roy and The Three Squires. This was a definite success, making 50% more income than the previous year's pantomime held at the Knightstone Theatre, and leaving everyone who saw it full of praise.

With The Playhouse now back up and running after a five-year wait, the town of Weston finally had its home of entertainment back.

The Theatre Club

Every theatre needs support to keep it going, from companies who perform there, staff members and members of the public who make up the audiences; but extra support can also come from volunteers, and so in 1969 the Weston-super-Mare Theatre Club, which later became The Playhouse Theatre Club, was formed.

The aim of the club was for members to assist in building up regular audiences at both The Playhouse and Knightstone theatres, as well as other entertainment venues in the town and to also suggest future programmes.

It was said by the Catering and Entertainments Committee that 'we have to try and involve the local residents as much as possible', and so the inaugural meeting was held at the Winter Gardens in May, attracting approximately 50 people. It was agreed that members – with a minimum age set at 15 – would pay a subscription of ten shillings a year and in return they would receive a newsletter and be invited to attend club activities. The club was invited to tour the new Playhouse in July 1969, and in 1970 they came up with the idea of holding a monthly Saturday coffee morning at the theatre in a bid to open it up to the public.

In 1972 the club boasted a membership of 300 at its annual general meeting, and it was reported that block bookings of shows had shown a good increase in support for The Playhouse. The membership continued to grow and by 1979 had reached 421, with a target of 500 being set for the next annual meeting.

Monthly meetings were held to which the club invited guest speakers, with the first being actor Simon Gard who gave an insight into the world of acting. The members were also treated to performances from amateur groups such as The Wayfarers, who entertained a full house with the comedy 'Women at War' in 1977 and one-act play 'Albert' in 1982.

The club started a tradition of inviting the cast of the summer shows to the coffee mornings to show them how members supported the theatre, and social events such as Christmas parties and skittles evenings were also held in a bid to create friendships between members and encourage people to meet.

Although the theatre club proved successful in boosting attendance at the town's theatres, in 1982 it faced difficulty when four vacancies were created during one meeting. The roles of Vice-Chairman, Honorary Secretary, Social Secretary and Membership Secretary were all up for replacement and needed to be filled urgently to ensure the continued smooth running of the club. It was hoped the gaps would be filled by other members, and although the club continued for another four years, it was forced to close in 1986 with the final meeting held on 4th July.

Lack of support was blamed for the closure, with the main reason being increasing difficulty in encouraging people to attend the theatre. It was mentioned that, as many members of the club were advancing in years, they were reluctant to go out in the evenings to attend shows, and therefore attendance at the theatre became lower and lower. There had also been an issue with decreasing numbers signing up for social trips.

Membership had fallen from the heights of nearly 500 to less than 100, and there had also been difficulty in getting people to serve on the committee. Therefore, approximately 16 years after it was formed to support the theatre, the club closed its doors, with the remaining assets of £250 being donated to the Sunshine Radio Appeal at Weston General Hospital.

During the following years, the theatre relied on public support more than ever; however, it wasn't long before another volunteer group was created – one which has raised nearly £250,000 for The Playhouse and is still going strong today: The Friends of The Playhouse.

The 1970s

With a newly modernised theatre now in place, The Playhouse continued to show its appeal with a variety of entertainment lined up following the pantomime that included amateur dramatic societies, opera and professional repertory as well as music concerts. It was noted in the local press that while the Knightstone Theatre used to be the focus of live entertainment, this was now being adequately catered for by The Playhouse.

While professional companies continued to entertain with dramas such as Agatha Christie's thriller 'Ten Little Niggers' (as it was known then – later revised to 'And Then There Were None') and Shakespeare's 'As You Like It', in March 1970 The Red Triangle Players set a new record for amateur societies when the 'house full' signs were displayed outside the theatre during two consecutive performances of their production of 'Pinocchio'. Experimenting with a children's play in the hope that performing for children would become a regular feature in their programmes, the society entertained over 2,500 audience members, with parties of children coming from as far as Warminster to see it.

Other amateur societies such as The Wayfarers and Weston-super-Mare Operatic Society also entertained audiences at the theatre before the summer season began, but on 25th May, The Playhouse had a flashback to the fire of 1964 when a fire broke out next door. Fifteen minutes after the audience had left the theatre, the alarm was raised at John Moore (Sports) Ltd when flames were spotted through the front display windows, prompting staff from the theatre to run out with their own hose reel to help. They also took fire extinguishers up onto the roof in an attempt to extinguish the flames, but the heat from inside the shop had already made the roof too hot to touch. Staff from the Winter Gardens also ran to help and stock from the theatre bar was moved in case the fire spread through the adjoining roofs, but thankfully, despite thick smoke filling the High Street, the fire was quickly contained by the fire brigade, who arrived on the scene promptly, and most of the damage was found to be in the display window where it was thought there had been an electrical fault.

Despite the trip down memory lane, The Playhouse was unaffected by the fire, and the council reported the income of the theatre since its re-opening being £14,400 above their estimate, even with the rise in expenditure.

Audiences continued to support the theatre, and on 22nd June, professional laughter show 'The Mating Game' arrived, starring Nicholas Parsons and Amanda Barrie (who would later become known to TV audiences as Alma Baldwin in 'Coronation Street'). Guaranteed to put a smile on the faces of the audience, it also satisfied those in charge, as every night it attracted a full house and, as the theatre reached its first anniversary, another successful season was predicted with the return of the Brian Rix Company taking up residence for the summer to entertain the town with 'Stand by your Bedouin'.

Returning to the theatre after his performance in 'Let Sleeping Wives Lie', Leo Franklyn praised The Playhouse, saying: 'It is beautiful from the point of view of the audience and actors. You only need to whisper on the stage and you can be heard at the back of the circle. The lighting too is the best I have ever seen.'

With the show proving to be a box office success, Basil Flavell expressed the view that although The Playhouse would take up to three years to build up a reputation, the programme for the summer season was one of the best in the country for a provincial theatre – a fact that was proved at the box office with many 'house full' signs having been on display.

*

The start of a new year brought a performance of a different kind from anything The Playhouse had hosted before when an appearance by 'King of the Witches' Alex Sanders, who claimed to be able to raise the devil, was scheduled to take place in February 1971. With plans for guards to be present to restrain his wife, who would be acting as high priestess, and any audience members with weak hearts warned to stay away, the show was definitely not family-friendly, and caused locals to speak out against it. Therefore, following protests from the local council and churches, it was announced seven days before it was due to be performed that, although the 'stage show' had no black magic or nudity in it, it would be moved to the Webbington Country Club, and people who had booked tickets for The Playhouse would be refunded. Despite the initial concerns by some, the announcement that the show was being forced to change venues came as a surprise. However, the theatre didn't suffer because of this and enjoyed a successful run of 'Puss in Boots' by The Red Triangle Players instead, just a year after they had set a box office record for their last children's performance.

*

David Jason and Bob Monkhouse having fun in 'She's Done it Again'.

The summer season of 1971 welcomed back the Brian Rix Company with 'She's Done it Again', starring Bob Monkhouse, Bill Treacher – who was spending his third summer in Weston – and a little-known theatre actor called David Jason. The farce provided lots of laughter as well as success at the box office as it was reported that most of the performances were more than three quarters full, with the matinees pulling in equally good audiences. The production also started a friendship between Bob and David as after performing together at The Playhouse they would go on to work together on Bob's radio show.

During the show, the two of them enjoyed each other's company so much that they would play around with their roles on stage – much to the ignorance of the audience. As part of his role, David would walk onto the stage with one of the newborn babies wrapped in a blanket and as the nights went on, he would make additions to the doll including adding a sausage to it in a rather rude way, as well as presenting Bob with just his underpants wrapped in the blanket!

In his autobiography David described working with Bob as a 'happy experience', and Bob was equally cheerful about their pairing in his. While watching Brian Rix in the role which he would take over, Bob wrote that he hadn't heard of David at the time, but that 'I met David during rehearsals and loved him on sight'. He also praised him as a performer, recalling how he was 'hysterical and acrobatic', and that 'he got a huge roar every night from the audience and the biggest ovation of the whole cast'.

Following the run, Bob asked David to work on his radio show 'Mostly Monkhouse', which ran for three series between 1972 and 1974 and received huge listening figures. Who would have thought that The Playhouse Theatre would play such a part in bringing two big showbiz figures together?

David clearly enjoyed his time performing at the theatre as he returned in October to star alongside Peter Adamson (Len Fairclough in 'Coronation Street') in a new comedy called 'Partners', which also brought in the laughs. As the year drew to a close, audiences were treated to performances from The Wayfarers and Weston-super-Mare Dramatic Society as well as Ballet Rambert, and demand was high for the annual pantomime, with bookings

The fun had by the cast during 'She's Done it Again'.

already 20% up on the previous year. It was later reported that an estimated 30,000 people watched the pantomime at the theatre, which was gaining a reputation for putting on a traditional show, and as Bunny Baron's production had broken box office records while providing value for money, it was recommended that he should continue to produce pantomimes for the theatre – a partnership which would last 17 years.

*

The next few years saw The Playhouse play to its strengths, hosting variety with professional companies taking their place in the programme alongside amateur societies and a mixture of seasonal and one-night performances. The Junior Arts Festival was also held at the theatre, and with well-known names such as Sue Nicholls, Bob Grant ('On the Buses'), Barbara Mullen ('Dr Finlay's Casebook') and Lesley Anne Down ('Upstairs Downstairs') taking their place on the stage, The Playhouse continued to entertain the public with box office records regularly being broken.

'No Sex Please, We're British' was performed at the theatre during the summer season of 1974, at the same time as its run at the Strand Theatre in London. It brought the West End to Weston as two extra rows of seats had to be installed due to its popularity, and Mr Jack Martin, Entertainments Officer for the council, said at the time: 'Without the slightest shadow of doubt, this is the best Playhouse season we have ever had'. He wasn't wrong as it was revealed that the comedy had smashed box office records and had set the bar high for the rest of the year. Mr Martin was quoted as saying: 'We have had a lot of people coming from a long way away. It has brought people into Weston who have now found they are within easy travelling distance of the theatre and we hope to do good business this autumn.'

This success continued for the rest of the year, causing Basil Flavell to reflect on the prediction he had made at the topping out ceremony for The Playhouse six years earlier in an interview with the local press. He said at the time:

> I sincerely believe that within five years we shall see the status and popularity of this new theatre grow to the point where it will not only make a significant

contribution to the life of the town, but will also be contributing to the loan charges.

He also recalled that, before the fire, The Playhouse had been a small theatre, producing approximately 21 weeks of acceptable repertory in the summer, a short panto run, and providing a home for amateur societies. Audiences had been around a few hundred per week. But now the town had a modern theatre open 52 weeks of the year, with professional plays of the highest standard attracting over 4,000 people per week and a summer season which attracted bigger numbers than before. The Playhouse was now regarded as one of the best provincial theatres in the country among the professional circles, and was known to a wide area with audiences coming from Cardiff, Swindon and even Birmingham.

However, he also said that, while 1974 had been a good year for the theatre, it would never show a profit as 'the public won't pay enough for their seats'. The introduction of films had contributed to the finances of the theatre and, with a wide programme of entertainment throughout the year, many people who attended often returned, but there was still work and effort to be done to maintain large audiences.

When he was asked if The Playhouse had made a significant contribution to the town of Weston he replied, 'Yes, we have reached that point. Can you imagine Weston without its Playhouse?' (I know I certainly can't.)

*

The summer season shows continued to prove their worth at The Playhouse when, in the summer of 1975, 'The Mating Game' was welcomed back to the theatre. Starring David Jason, Trevor Bannister ('Are You Being Served?') and Georgina Moon, the show helped Weston enjoy one of its best ever holiday seasons, with over 56,000 people attending to watch it. The good weather and high temperatures encouraged more visitors to the town, with The Playhouse, the Knightstone and the Rozel Gardens bandstand reportedly £10,000 up on the season's estimates.

'The Mating Game' was billed as a comedy, but one audience experienced a show not even the actors had planned on. During one performance, the cast experienced a mistiming of cues and, while the audience didn't know any different and laughed along with it, David Jason could do nothing but stand by and watch as drawers shot out from a filing cabinet, a bookcase slid around the stage and a table revolved all at the same time! Thankfully, the rest of the run went without a hitch, and David was more than complimentary when asked about his time at The Playhouse, saying: 'I've heard what your old theatre was like. It's lucky you've got such a splendid theatre now.' He also said the theatre was comfortable adding 'that's the best thing you can say about a theatre really.'

Success returned to the theatre in the summer of 1976, with Trevor Bannister also returning to perform in the comedy 'A Bit between the Teeth', written by Michael Pertwee, but in 1977 the summer season underwent an experiment and, instead of having one summer show, there was a proposal to have two.

Due to the withdrawal of the company who had been responsible for the summer shows during the past few years, it was decided by a new company that two shows could be held during the lucrative summer season, with comedy 'Let's Do it Your Way', starring real-life married couple Liza Goddard and Colin Baker, chosen for the first part of the season, and 'Two and Two Make Sex', starring Ian Lavender and Henry McGee, for the second. But while this decision was deemed risky, the experiment paid off, with Mr Jack Martin quoted as saying: 'It has gone extremely well and we are highly satisfied with the financial result. The Playhouse is doing much better than last year.'

It proved such a success that this format continued for the next two years with 'Caught on the Hop', running from 26th June to 5th August 1978, starring Frances de la Tour and Trevor Bannister, and 'Fringe Benefits' running from 7th August to 23rd September, starring Christopher Blake ('Mixed Blessings') and Paul Greenwood ('The Growing Pains of PC Penrose' and 'Rosie').

'Who Goes Bare' with Robin Askwith ran from 25th June to 21st July 1979, followed by 'An Evening with Michael Parkinson' and 'An Evening with Diana Dors', but while it was reported that 25,000 people had visited The Playhouse since early June that year, not being able to get named stars in a

Weston Operatic Society's production of 'The Music Man'.
Photograph courtesy of Weston Operatic Society.

long-running play during the season had impacted on attendances, and another change for the summer season of 1980 was suggested to the council. However, the comedy 'Don't Just Lie There, Say Something' starring Jack Douglas ('Carry On' films), Bill Pertwee, Cardew Robinson and Nicholas Smith ('Are You Being Served?') brought the laughter back to the theatre in October 1979, and was followed by performances from The Red Triangle Players, The Wayfarers and Weston-super-Mare Dramatic Society, before a staging of the pantomime 'Cinderella' starring real-life ponies brought the year to a close.

*

So, while professional productions were making the tills ring in the box office, it was up to the amateur societies to raise their game as well, and they didn't disappoint. With expectations high from audiences, Weston Operatic Society took on their most ambitious production in May 1975 when they performed 'The Music Man'. Costing £5,000 to put on and boasting a cast of 60 people, they needed 85% of tickets to be sold in order to break even, which they hoped to achieve as they were performing over a bank holiday.

The Wayfarers also stepped up when they performed 'Tom Jones', their most ambitious production, for their 20th anniversary performance in April 1976, and Weston-super-Mare Operatic Society took on a costly and ambitious production when they performed 'The Pajama Game' in April 1977 with a cast of 80 people.

None of the efforts of the amateur societies went unrecognised, and audiences supported them as much as the professional shows. From dramas to musicals and comic operettas, their efforts didn't disappoint, but the greatest reward came at Easter 1978 when Weston Operatic Society's production of 'Gigi' –which was the premiere of the amateur production in the West of England – became their first major show in four years to make a profit. Costing £7,000 to put on – their most expensive production – the society really raised the bar, hoping to attract audiences of 91% in order to make a profit. They achieved this, hitting 92%, and in the process raised money for multiple sclerosis charities during a gala opening night.

Film Theatre

In early 1971, the idea of showing films at the
theatre was discussed by the Borough Council,
with one councillor expressing the view that it would
be 'another financial disaster' and that it would mean 'bringing in a declining
art to help another declining art'. It was questioned whether people would want
to attend the theatre to watch a film when there were two cinemas in the town,
as well as films being shown on TV.

However, in March, the Borough Council's Catering and Entertainments
Committee agreed to fund £10,500 towards the cost of building a projection room
and installing equipment to allow The Playhouse to show films during the winter
period when takings were poor. It was estimated that the cost of the projection
room would be £5,000 and the equipment would cost £10,000, although it was
hoped that a subsidy of £7,500 would be provided by the British Film Institute.

It was intended that the theatre would show different films from those on
general release to encourage more people to attend. It was pointed out by Basil
Flavell, the Corporation General Manager, that the idea of a projection room
had been included in the original plans of the theatre, as well as in the plans for
the rebuilt theatre following the fire, but had been cut to provide a saving and
also to allow as much time as possible for live theatre. Despite this, it was now
agreed that the idea should go ahead, allowing films to be shown at the theatre
along with the other forms of entertainment audiences enjoyed.

In December it was reported that the British Film Institute had yet to make a
decision about whether to provide a grant to go towards the projection room,
and therefore work couldn't go ahead without this. The Institute was quoted at
the time as saying that Weston was 'categorically at the top of the list in consideration for a grant', but it wasn't until January 1972 that it finally made its decision.
The British Film Institute made a grant of £10,000 towards the equipment, and
it was hoped that work on the projection room would be completed by the end
of March, so that screenings could take place as early as June.

In May 1972 the theatre was granted a cinema licence which would finally allow
them to show films – and it did so for the next 15 years.

The Projector.
Photograph courtesy of James Gentle.

With the theatre expanding its appeal to a wider audience, the introduction of films meant that theatre staff had to be trained as projectionists in order to use the equipment. A projection screen was installed at the theatre weighing quite a bit heavier than anticipated, and a Children's Film Festival, a six-week season of children's films arranged by the Children's Film Foundation, was put together to coincide with the school summer holidays. Aimed at children between five and 15 years old, a variety of films was shown every morning, and repeated every couple of weeks to ensure children didn't miss out on a particular film. General screening of films started from 18th September, with the opening film, 'Modern Times' starring Charlie Chaplin, chosen in association with the British Film Institute.

So, The Playhouse was now being used as a film theatre as well as continuing with live performances. The Children's Film Festival proved a success as attendances steadily increased over the weeks and averaged at about 200 per screening, and by the end of 1972, the film theatre was being praised by those who attended it as well as staff who worked there.

In May 1973 it had its first sold-out screening – 'The Golden Age of Steam' – with over 90% of the seats booked in advance, showing that the introduction of films had been a success. It was reported that the screening of films was increasing the revenue of the theatre, which helped to provide more live entertainment.

Over the years the film theatre proved very popular, providing entertainment to audiences during 'dark days' when no live performances took place, and it also encouraged people who wouldn't necessarily think of attending the theatre to see what was on offer. A variety of comedy, drama and family films were shown.

One lady recalled to me her memory of watching 'Jaws' in her role as usherette at the theatre:

> As an usherette you have to sit in on performances to keep an eye on and be there for the audiences. Being able to see shows and films is a perk of the job, but can become boring when you see things multiple times. When the movie 'Jaws' was released, I gave into the boredom after seeing it a few times and threw pieces of ice-cream cone into the auditorium every time the shark made its appearance to give the audience more of a reason to jump!

In 1997, the Weston-super-Mare Film Society was set up, with the aim being to provide a varied programme at the theatre and also for members of the society to have a say in what was to be shown. Films chosen by the society were shown one day per month during two half-yearly programmes and were also open to the public. But unfortunately in early 2014, the society was informed that when the current season ended, it would no longer be able to show films at the theatre. Low attendances on dates when 'stronger theatrical offerings could be held' were blamed, and the society agreed that the theatre had in fact lost money due to showing films. It was also reported that as films were going digital, it would cost £80,000 to install a new system at the theatre. As there were no funds available to accommodate this, it was decided it wasn't financially viable to continue and the use of the projection equipment was discontinued.

Pete Magor told me:

> We stopped showing films when everything went over to digital as it was more complicated. We used to receive the film on a hard drive in the post which we had to download and then you'd send it on to the next cinema. As fewer films became available in a 35mm format, it became too expensive to run.

Despite not being used any more, the projection equipment remains in the box at the rear of the circle (which is also home to the follow spot – a bright spotlight used to highlight either a certain performer or part of the stage during a performance), as a reminder of a time gone by, and although it is rarely used nowadays, it doesn't look as out of date as I thought it might.

The 1980s: Variety is the Spice of Life

The success of any theatre relies on the support of the public attending shows, and to ensure as wide an audience as possible, a mix of entertainment keeps interest high. So, while The Playhouse may have been originally created to provide plays and repertory theatre, variety in the programme has always been key, and this was clear as The Playhouse entered a new decade.

With the summer already set to focus on comedy and family fun with 'The Keith Harris Spectacular' booked for the season, The Playhouse didn't shy away from attracting as many different forms of entertainment as it could to boost diversity, starting with the debut of The Oxford Playhouse Company, who presented the three-act play 'Absurd Person Singular' in March 1980.

Pop duo Peters and Lee, along with special guests, provided a one-night-only performance in April, and June became the month of comedy 'show' weeks, with 'The Charlie Bennett Show', 'The Roger Kitter Show' and 'The Lennie Bennett Show' warming up the audiences, before Keith Harris, Cuddles and Orville, along with Des King and The Duanes, provided a summer of what audience members described as 'more than a show – it's an experience'. Audiences spread the word about the variety and entertainment value of the show, resulting in each performance having only a handful of seats left for the next day.

The decision to stage a variety show during the summer broke the tradition of a play season, but paid off, as it was recorded as the best ever summer show at the theatre, and played its part in providing Weston with its most successful summer season ever. Thirty-seven performances were completely sold out, and attendance was over 98% at the rest, bringing fun and laughter to the town.

Frankie Vaughan made an appearance at the theatre, entertaining audiences for two performances in October, before films such as 'Blazing Saddles' and 'The Deep' were shown in the run-up to Christmas, when the pantomime of 'Sleeping Beauty' also boosted the success of the theatre by providing the box office with a new record. Mr Jack Martin was delighted with the public reaction to the pantomime and was quoted as saying that he felt 'this one is as good as we have ever had'.

*

While the theatre continued to provide appreciative audiences with entertainment, the building itself required some care and attention when it was revealed in February 1981 that the decorative windows in the bar area would need to be removed due to the wooden frames naturally rotting. An estimated cost of £7,000 was put forward, but the true cost would be revealed once the windows were removed and work started on replacing the frames. However, this work was delayed, not taking place until May 1982, and ended up costing a total of £11,000.

The windows weren't the only changes being made to the theatre, as a new hearing system was installed in June 1981, as part of the Year of the Disabled, which would allow hearing aids to pick up on magnetic waves in the theatre and therefore enhance the experience for those hard of hearing. The system was set up by theatre managers Tony Blizzard and Pete Magor – who built the amplifier himself – and consisted of a loop of wire being installed around the auditorium. Advice from the Horizon Hard of Hearing Club was sought, and club members were given the opportunity to test the new system when they attended a matinee performance of 'Tomb with a View' by The Red Triangle Players in November. Hailed as a great success, the system was only available for those in the stalls, but it was hoped it would be extended to the circle in time for the start of the pantomime.

The installation of this system prompted consideration for disabled patrons unable to use the stairs whose only means of accessing the auditorium at the time was being carried by staff. It was acknowledged that a stairlift was urgently needed; however, the biggest focus on disabled access within the theatre didn't take place until 1995.

*

While the building itself was being taken care of, the theatre continued to keep audiences laughing throughout 1981, with a focus on comedy including 'The Bernie Winters Show' and 'The Bernie Clifton Show', before 'The Jerry Stevens Show' took up residence for a season filled with laughter and song. Nevertheless, the recession and good weather didn't help indoor entertainment, and family fun shows weren't enough to entice people to attend The Playhouse or the Winter Gardens, which both reported a disappointing season.

The weather was also to blame when four performances of 'Jack and the Beanstalk' were cancelled due to snow and ice at the end of the year. The pantomime, which had seen the highest advance bookings of all time, boasted nearly double the figures for the first week of the new year than those for the same week of the previous year, and, despite the cancelled shows, The Playhouse pantomime once again achieved a record number of audience members, with 34 of the 51 performances boasting higher attendances than the previous year.

*

While the weather hadn't done much damage to panto takings, it clearly wasn't quite ready to give up, as in February 1982, audience members were treated to a continuation of the icy set of 'The Snow Queen' when real snow began to fall as they left the theatre after the performance.

Following the run of devastating weather during the winter, which caused flooding and damage to properties in the town, a number of concerts were held at The Playhouse at the start of the year to aid the Weston Flood Relief fund. With audiences digging deep to raise money for those affected, the concerts proved a success and as the weather started to improve, the theatre continued with its mix of entertainment.

With great support from the public, 'The Tom O'Connor Show' was performed

Weston Operatic Society's production of 'Half a Sixpence'.
Photograph courtesy of Weston Operatic Society.

in March, followed by Iris Williams and her musicians appearing in April. Weston Operatic Society's production of 'Half a Sixpence' was staged during Easter Week, but unfortunately it didn't receive the houses it deserved and it was reported that the society was likely to lose approximately £1,000 due to this.

Despite this disappointment, with the summer season approaching, a number of shows brought the theatre to local attention with a six-week repertory season held from 4th May, with plays that included 'Rebecca', 'Death Trap' and 'Boeing Boeing', followed by 'The Rupert Show' for children, and concerts by The Yetties and The Syd Lawrence Orchestra.

Once again, the format of the summer season was changed, with a variety of one-night shows taking place during the week and films being shown at the end of the week. This summer season provided a number of well-known names, such as Des O'Connor – who returned to Weston for the first time since topping the bill at the Knightstone Theatre in 1957, Lonnie Donegan, Larry Grayson, Brotherhood of Man, Ted Rogers, Val Doonican and Ken

Dodd (who would later become patron of The Friends) with their debut performances at The Playhouse. The 23-year-old comedian Lenny Henry, who was known to TV audiences for appearing on 'Tiswas', also made his first appearance, performing two shows which proved so successful that, less than a month after his debut, he was invited back again. Unfortunately, however, a combination of the World Cup, Wimbledon, the Falklands War and the recession meant that, although the theatre had one of its best summer seasons in terms of entertainment, overall numbers were lower than expected, resulting in income for the theatre being £51,434 under target. It was said that if this style of summer season were to continue, there would be more emphasis on live entertainment and fewer films would be shown, as it was thought that closing the week with films may have made people stay away at peak times.

While the disappointment of the summer sank in, doubts about the future of summer entertainment at The Playhouse's rival theatre the Knightstone were being expressed, as it was commented that although open for only 14 weeks of the year, considerable repairs were needed to the building in order for it to continue being used. But the question was raised whether, with The Playhouse providing most of the entertainment in the town, there was a need for the Knightstone Theatre any more.

With The Playhouse box office already busy with advance bookings for panto, Keith Harris returned to the theatre with friends Orville and Cuddles in November to warm up audiences, two years after his summer season had achieved a record run. Welcomed back with open arms, his appearance was followed by Harry Corbett and Sooty, who kept audiences laughing, until Weston Dramatic Society performed 'Pardon Me Prime Minister' in early December, and the panto season began.

*

With 'Little Red Riding Hood' still pulling in the crowds in the early part of 1983, the success of its run prompted the council to announce the following year's panto as 'Cinderella' and that it would run from Boxing Day for five weeks. Although there had been fewer performances, 'Little Red Riding Hood' had attracted nearly a thousand more people to the theatre than the previous year, and higher ticket prices had helped to boost the theatre's income. It was noted that, although all pantomimes appeal to families, 'Little Red Riding Hood' had had a particularly special appeal for children.

*

In an attempt to reach out to visitors further afield, at the start of the year, The Playhouse enlisted the help of agents who could book tickets for shows on their behalf. Visitors to the theatre who lived in rural areas had expressed difficulty in booking as attending the theatre before shows wasn't always practical, and so a variety of venues were chosen as agents in areas such as Clevedon, Backwell and Winscombe, in the hope that people who lived outside the local area wouldn't miss out.

As a sweetener for those who could now book tickets without having to attend the theatre, a season of variety was on the cards for the summer, and 'big name' performers were announced as early as March. No one could deny the theatre's efforts to provide the town with a spectacular line-up, as the bill could easily have been that for a top variety show, but it also proved the theatre was speaking for itself, as return visits from Des O'Connor, Lenny Henry and Ken Dodd were planned. Ken's shows the previous year had given audience members value for money as they had both run over time. Although complaints had been made to the theatre by people waiting to see his 8.30pm performance, Playhouse Manager Tony Blizzard commented, 'No one can control Ken Dodd. If he wants to carry on he does!', and when he was asked to finish his earlier show by 8pm, Mr Blizzard recalled that 'he just laughed', which resulted in his later performance over-running by two hours!

But despite the amazing line-up, the rising costs of promotion and the opening of the Tropicana in May were blamed for The Playhouse ending the season with another loss, as many visitors were distracted by the new venue and its facilities, including a swimming pool.

Summer Season Line-up, 1983

26th June	The English Philharmonic Orchestra: 'A Strauss Family Gala Evening'
30th June	Tom O'Connor
1st & 2nd July	Ken Dodd
3rd July	Humphrey Lyttleton
7th July	Gerry & the Pacemakers
8th & 9th July	Vince Hill
14th - 16th July	Cilla Black
17th July	Jack Fear Big Bang: 'An Evening of Glenn Miller Music'
21st - 23rd July	Max Bygraves
28th - 30th July	Harry Secombe
3rd & 4th August	Des O'Connor
5th & 6th August	Lenny Henry
11th - 13th August	Tommy Cooper
17th & 18th August	Sacha Distel
19th & 20th August	Iris Williams
25th - 27th August	Jim Davidson
28th August	The Great Western Chorus: 'A Barbershop Evening'
1st September	Pam Ayres
2nd & 3rd September	Val Doonican

However, better news was on the way when two performances by Freddie Starr in November sold out, and it was announced that more amateur societies were to be given permission to perform at the theatre during the spring and autumn seasons. This meant that amateur productions would take up 14 more weeks during the year, which some felt could cut into the performance time of professional artists, but Mr Clive Jackson, Director of Leisure and Tourism, defended this decision, saying: 'This could create criticism from both visitor and resident theatre patrons, but it is my view that local amateur societies do create a considerable interest in live theatre and the arts within the district.'

So, while amateur societies were being given more space in the programme, would this result in the theatre attracting fewer well-known names? The answer to this question was thankfully 'no', as the summer season of 1984 was announced just as early as the previous year, with performers such as Little and Large, Cilla Black (who subsequently had to cancel following doctor's orders), Max Bygraves, Tommy Cooper and Ken Dodd already booked to appear. With the line-up already looking impressive, Mr Jack Martin, Woodspring's Entertainments Manager, said: 'I can safely say no resort in the country will have a better line-up this summer. We are bringing back the people who were successful last summer.' While many of the performers were returning to the theatre, negotiations were also ongoing to attract many new names to the line-up, with hopes being held out for The Nolans – who consequently filled Tommy Cooper's place in the programme following his death three weeks before he was due to appear.

*

In addition to attempting to attract star performers to the theatre, thoughts turned to other ways the public could be encouraged to attend. The idea of an open day was hit upon by local producers Nona Hooper and Bill Clout as a way of publicising the theatre, and it was agreed by Jack Martin that free tours would be advertised during which members of the public would be given the opportunity to see the theatre's inner workings. A performance called 'Playhouse Presents', aimed at showcasing the variety of performances The Playhouse could present, was also arranged for the evening, with tickets priced at 50p.

By throwing open the doors to the public, it was hoped that people would see that there is more to the theatre than just a stage, and it would show how the different areas within the theatre all work together to produce shows. House Manager Tony Blizzard was optimistic about the tours and was quoted as saying: 'We are trying to find ways of attracting people to the theatre who perhaps have not been before. We want to generate more interest in The Playhouse.'

The idea of the tours definitely did generate interest as, within a number of weeks, all of the tours were fully booked, and a further two tours were scheduled. However, there was disappointment for theatre managers when fewer than half of the people who had pre-booked turned up, while others had had to be turned away as tickets had sold out. The tours were guided by Tony Blizzard and Pete Magor and covered the backstage area, committee room, dressing rooms and the projection room, as well as the mechanics of the stage including the lighting and sound boards.

Despite the disappointment, nearly 500 people attended the evening show with Mr Jack Martin quoted as saying: 'The intention was to win some new customers for The Playhouse. I think it did the theatre a lot of good and was well worth doing.'

An open day including free tours of the theatre was something The Friends of The Playhouse would later take on as part of their role in supporting and promoting the theatre.

*

As the summer season continued to follow the tradition of a mix of shows instead of one show for the whole summer, which had started in 1982, Mr Martin said:

> Having big names for short runs gives us the opportunity to attract the public and encourage those who do come to come again and again. With The Playhouse seating capacity, it is crucial that people come along to pay for these expensive artistes.

Jim Davidson is congratulated on his full houses.

Support was indeed high, with four out of six performances by Jim Davidson selling out, making him the most popular entertainer to visit the town in the last two years. Not one to be outdone, the legendary Ken Dodd, who was celebrating his 30th year in show business, returned to the theatre in July with three sold-out shows and put himself firmly back on top with the public.

Making his debut for one night only during a break from his season in Ilfracombe, Irish comedian Frank Carson also appeared at The Playhouse in August 1984, following The Nolan Sisters and the 'The Showaddywaddy Show', as well as comedian Duncan Norvelle.

With a great line-up of entertainers appearing at The Playhouse, it was noted that the theatre was able to advertise its shows nationally, which in turn meant wider publicity for the theatre as well as the town of Weston. Comedian Frankie Howerd also helped to bring The Playhouse to the attention of the nation when he chose the theatre as a venue to film his TV show for Channel 4 in April 1986. Performing for two nights in front of an invited audience, this TV special marked his return to television following a five-year absence, and opened the doors for more comedy at the theatre with Stan Boardman, Bobby Davro, Gary Wilmot, The Krankies, and Rod Hull and Emu set to appear during the summer.

*

As part of a new policy by the council, The Playhouse returned to the traditional summer show for 1987, with 'Bernie Clifton's Holiday Laughter Show' set to entertain audiences for a ten-week season. Supported by comedy act Mini Tones (made up of 'Star Wars' actor Kenny Baker and his partner Jack), singer Michelle Breeze, dancing girl group Panache and The Tim Sweet Band, the summer was set for another festival of fun, with Ken Dodd also returning, as well as Hale & Pace treading the boards to a full house. The value of entertainment was high, but unfortunately by the summer of 1988, the variety of entertainment was reduced to a handful of shows, with films taking up the majority of the programme. This resulted in the fear that the theatre may be losing its way, with big names no longer featuring as prominently in the programme as they once did.

Hard Times

The late 1980s to early 1990s were hard times for The Playhouse as, following a loss of £13,930, Woodspring District Council officials pulled advertising from the *Weston Mercury* (formerly *Weston Mercury & Somerset Herald*) for a month following the summer season of 1989 in a bid to save money. A lack of support and hot weather were blamed for the loss, and the council reported a drop of £25,000 below target, when a profit of £6,500 had been forecast.

While local societies called the lack of advertising 'a crying shame', Weston Dramatic Society, who had just started performing '84 Charing Cross Road' at the theatre, put in a bid for compensation from the council as they blamed the lack of advertising for the loss they experienced. Chairman of the Society John Butler said: 'We were annoyed that we did not get any warning that Woodspring were pulling out their advertising.' Deputy Leisure Director Gary Twinn was quoted at the time as saying: 'We are in discussions with the Dramatic Society about compensation because they feel their show takings were affected by the fact we did not advertise their production in the *Mercury*.' He said they would be the only society to receive compensation as 'They are the only ones who had a show which coincided with our pulling out of *Mercury* advertising.'

Other plans being made to save money included cutting the budget for the theatre by £50,000 during 1991-92, with subsequent year's cuts set to potentially total £80,000, but concerns were expressed that this would downgrade the entertainment value provided at the theatre to the extent that it would no longer be an attraction.

Although the theatre was running at a loss, the Mayor of Weston, Councillor Mike Wedlake, hit out at that the way the theatre was being run and slammed Woodspring Council for piling council costs onto The Playhouse budget. Calling for a rethink on the type of entertainment provided at the theatre, he said:

> Some of the big names which have been coming to The Playhouse cost too much and some of the material could not be called a family show. Big names often draw crowds but can be financial disasters. We want Weston to be a quality resort and need quality performances without high prices.

He also expressed his support for the amateur societies, when he commented 'It is not the local amateur groups which drain the resources', but in an attempt to increase profits, the theatre increased the charges for amateur societies from a minimum of £195 per week to £600, with musical societies facing a minimum fee of £1,000. There were further increases in 1991 when the minimum fee was increased to £800 per week, and rehearsal nights were also charged for, bringing the minimum charge up to approximately £2,000. It was noted that when the theatre was rebuilt, there had been a big emphasis on the need for local societies to be supported to perform at the theatre, but local groups now hit out, claiming that increasing the charges could have the opposite effect and result in fewer people attending the theatre. The changes caused further outrage when it was announced that they would come into effect halfway through the year, meaning that only two societies would face the higher rates while the others would pay the previous charge for one more production.

A meeting was held between the council and societies in a bid to discuss the new arrangements, but unfortunately the charges couldn't be reduced, as it was reported that the theatre had to make savings of £50,000 throughout the year. This resulted in many groups no longer being able to perform there, and therefore the productions of both Weston Dramatic Society and Reflections held in April 1991 would be their last at the theatre. With the situation described as 'delicate', The Red Triangle Players and The Wayfarers decided to consider their futures with The Playhouse later in the year.

*

A 'complete review' of The Playhouse was promised by new Entertainments Officer Alan Bowler when he took up his role in early 1991, and in April of that year a three-year action plan was put in place by Woodspring Council. In an attempt to ensure a bright financial future for the theatre and prevent it from becoming a 'black hole for money', it was decided to continue the council subsidy of £200,000 per year and that an emphasis should be placed on improving the quality of the programme as well as improving marketing.

To increase bookings, a decision was made to issue vouchers giving £2 off a ticket for touring production 'Murder in Mind' in February 1991 owing to low bookings, but this didn't go down well with regular theatre-goers, who complained about missing out as they had booked in advance. Mr Bowler fed back that the decision 'may not be a one-off and could be introduced for future shows if advance bookings aren't high enough'.

An experimental new system of ticket prices was also trialled in an attempt to increase sales. Not to be used for all shows, the aim was to provide the best seats people could afford, and so 'gold', 'silver' and 'bronze' seats were introduced, with prices staggered depending on the location of the seats. However, the public soon expressed concern that, despite the varying prices, they had been raised to such an extent that families could only afford to buy the cheaper seats at the rear of the theatre. Although the prices remained lower than other venues, it seemed this wasn't the main issue, with Councillor John Wiltshire quoted as saying 'the trouble is local people do not support it'.

In August – 15 weeks into the action plan – it was reported that so far it had been a success, with audiences increased by 28% and gross takings doubled compared to the same period of the previous year. The formation of The Friends had helped to boost audiences, with membership steadily climbing, but a member of the public expressed doubts about the group, querying in a letter to the *Weston Mercury* 'whether members of the club would be encouraged to attend the theatre any more often than they would have already done'. In a positive response to this, it was reported that over 250 people had joined The Friends to play an active role within the organisation, and that the coffee mornings each Saturday had proved successful. The Friends had also, within a few short months, organised voluntary front-of-house staff, a poster distribution team, frequent mailshots and guided theatre tours, as well as a supper club for members.

Bob Acland, Woodspring's Director of Marketing and Distribution, also praised the efforts of The Friends, as well as the theatre, when he said:

> The Friends group has been formed and now has 250 members. Market research has also been carried out to find out what local people want to see at The Playhouse. Advertising material has been completely revamped and I believe we are starting to win the battle. We need to make a dramatic impact this year. A great deal of energy has gone into this plan because it is vitally important to Weston.

Despite reports that the theatre was still losing money and hadn't hit the £50,000 savings target, an open day held in November 1991 proved a success, with over 400 people attending the event and membership of The Friends receiving a boost. However, calls were made in early 1992 to shut the theatre as it was costing £250,000 a year to run and, despite improved attendance figures, profits were plummeting. A suggestion was put forward for the theatre to become a charitable trust or to be run by a private company, but it was noted that arrangements for this could take a couple of years to be put in place, and action was needed sooner.

Sponsors were sought to help to counter the continued losses and, while the programme for local productions during the year had already been filled, a survey completed by the public during the summer revealed that supporters of The Playhouse would like to see headline acts perform. With this in mind, Tom O'Connor was booked to appear every Sunday during the summer presenting his popular TV game show 'Name That Tune', and Jethro and Ken Dodd were also lined up for return visits.

The theatre also received a lifeline from the Bristol Old Vic, who agreed to bring their own productions to the theatre as well as provide workshops during the 'dark season' – between the end of the pantomime and the start of the spring season – with the hope that this agreement could last up to four years. Yet even with this agreement in place, 'big name' acts lined up to appear in the autumn of 1992 such as Bob Geldof, Barbara Windsor and Rick Wakeman were cut after the theatre was described as being in the 'worst financial crisis for nearly 35 years'.

*

While the auditorium was mainly used for evening performances, an idea was put together to use the bar area for various activities during the day in an effort to use the theatre as much as possible, and so keep-fit and ballet classes for adults, as well as exhibitions by local organisations, were held. A café area aptly named 'Prompt Corner' was also created, providing tea, coffee and pastries to the public, but unfortunately this venture was short-lived and it closed soon after opening.

The Playhouse was on everyone's minds as no one wanted to see it fail, and it was even mentioned in the inauguration speech of Mayor Peter Bryant in May 1992, when he urged locals to 'rally round to pump life back into the town's struggling Playhouse' which he described as one of the town's most important venues. As part of increasing awareness of the theatre, a new computerised system was installed in the revamped box office to enable information regarding upcoming shows to be circulated to interested patrons, and Woodspring's Marketing Committee promised better adver-tising for the theatre. In a special interview given to the *Weston Mercury*, Councillor Bob Thompson, Chairman of the Marketing Committee, gave a rousing speech on how the committee would continue to fight for the resort town of Weston, saying:

> I accept wholeheartedly that not everything I have done personally has come off, although I hope that most of it will bring back our theatre to its original glory in the next few months. We, like everyone else, have had a hard and difficult season due in the main to the recession; however, our brochure requests from all the country have risen by over 17% and our marketing department has been fighting for four years to ensure Weston retains its image as one of the best resorts in the country. We shall continue to do so as long as there is breath in our bodies.

In spite of the financial pressure on the theatre, good news was on its way when Ken Dodd's 'Laughter Show' was performed on 5th August to a full house, setting new box office records for a show by a single artist, proving that while The Playhouse may have been down, it was certainly not beaten.

＊

While the future of The Playhouse had been up in the air, it was decided in 1994 that Woodspring Council would retain control of the theatre and continue to subsidise it at the cost of £250,000 per year. New life was breathed into the theatre when a shake-up of staff created two new roles, with Alan Bowler being appointed as General Manager and Robbie Burns becoming the Marketing Manager. As part of an attempt to provide audiences with a warm welcome, all staff members took part in customer care training and also completed a Welcome Host course, with Alan Bowler saying: 'Our aim is to make The Playhouse one of the best theatres in this part of the world.'

The new management team continued their focus to boost the profile of the theatre, supporting a successful membership drive for The Friends of The Playhouse in the hope that numbers could top 500. As membership increased, Chairman of The Friends Ken Tapley thanked everyone for their support, while reflecting on the recent position of the theatre, saying: 'We want a theatre here and unless we all support it we stand a chance of losing it, although I don't think that's the case at the moment.'

As the 25th anniversary of the new theatre approached, a double celebration was in order. The Red Triangle Players celebrated their 70th birthday with a performance of 'Run for your Wife' in June, while in July Danny La Rue was a special guest at the theatre celebrations when he helped to unveil a commemorative plaque before performing during the evening. Councillor Ken Lacey, who also took part in the celebrations, cut the cake and looked to the future when he said: 'Anybody who is anybody in the world of show business has been here at some stage. The last few years have been rather difficult, but things are beginning to improve.'

With the theatre on the up, over the next few years the management team were praised as attendance numbers increased and income targets were reached and even beaten. Audiences remained entertained, with perform-ances from Bob Monkhouse, Ken Dodd, and Danny La Rue, as well as

The Friends of the Playhouse

presented this plaque to celebrate
the theatre's 25th Anniversary.

**It was unveiled by Councillor Ken Lacey
Chairman of Woodspring District Council and
Danny La Rue on Saturday 9th July 1994.**

Plaque to celebrate the
25th anniversary of the
new Playhouse.
Author's photograph.

Freddie Starr and Elkie Brooks, and in November 1996, theatre fans were
praised when every show of the Bruce James Production of 'Me and My Girl'
were sold out. General Manager Murray MacDonald said at the time:

> I am delighted with both the production of 'Me and My Girl' and the
> audience reaction to it. I have now booked the company for another four
> shows in 1997. North Somerset deserves the best in professional entertain-
> ment and now that we are building our reputation for professional musicals,
> it would be nice to do the same with drama.

As audiences continued to support the theatre with the summer season of
1997 boasting good old-fashioned entertainment including Ken Dodd, Little
and Large, Rod Hull and Emu, as well as Chas & Dave and Jethro, ambitious
plans to expand the theatre were put together by theatre bosses. As well as
upgrading facilities including the bar area, dressing rooms and the stairlift
as part of a £6 million extension scheme, the theatre submitted a £300,000
bid to the National Lottery in the hope of being able to work with architects
to draw up plans for the next stage of the ambitious project. This stage would
include expanding the theatre into six neighbouring properties which would
be used as offices, extra rehearsal rooms, a restaurant, dance studio and
meeting rooms, as well as a cinema.

General Manager Murray MacDonald who was to oversee the project said:

> It is our aim to build an education resource centre in a redeveloped theatre
> providing more space which can be used by all parts of the community. This
> development will much better serve the people of North Somerset.

However, this bid was unsuccessful so a second was submitted in the summer of 1998, but recent changes at the Arts Council had meant that the future for capital bids was unclear and unfortunately the theatre didn't receive the funding it needed for the major project it had hoped to put in place.

*

While the theatre wasn't able to expand as it had hoped, a controversial decision made by the council in early 1998 caused conflict between the theatre and amateur groups. With the council deciding to reduce its subsidy for amateur productions by cutting its community support grant by 20%, it meant that groups faced inflated hire charges, and meant that some, such as The Red Triangle Players, were no longer able to perform at the theatre.

With history repeating itself, as increased charges had been a matter of controversy seven years previously, a forum organised by the *Weston Mercury* was held to discuss the souring relationship between the theatre and local amateur groups. Issues raised included money lost from low ticket sales as amateur performances had been scheduled next to professional productions, the hire charges increasing by 20% and a lack of help for amateurs, while it was noted that the theatre owed a lot of its success to the past efforts of the amateur productions. General Manager Murray MacDonald attended the meeting on behalf of the theatre to try and smooth things over, reassuring everyone that the groups weren't being pushed out, saying:

> No one is being driven out, we make informed decisions about how much the theatre costs to run and how many tickets groups can sell. We are forgetting the brilliant venue we have here. Amateur use is less than 25% in terms of audiences coming to the theatre.

Closing the forum, Mr MacDonald acknowledged the importance of the amateur groups, saying: 'There will always be space for the amateurs in The Playhouse. They are a vital part of the theatre's work'. But unfortunately the increased charges still forced many groups to cease performing at the theatre.

Amateur Societies at The Playhouse

Over the years many amateur societies have performed at The Playhouse Theatre, including The Red Triangle Players, The Wayfarers and Weston Dramatic Society, and while hire prices have been a hot topic for discussion more than once during the history of the theatre, there are two societies that have continued to perform at the theatre up to this day: **Weston Operatic Society** (WOS) and **Worle Operatic & Dramatic Society** (WODS).

Formed in the early 1900s, WOS have performed at The Playhouse since the 1960s, and more recently up to twice a year, during Easter week and also in the autumn. The society have enjoyed performing a variety of shows, including Gilbert & Sullivan's 'Yeoman of the Guard', 'The Pirates of Penzance' and 'The Mikado', while in recent years, they have branched out into more modern musicals such as 'Annie', 'Legally Blonde' and 'Spamalot'.

During the summer seasons of the 1990s, the society were requested by the council to entertain holiday-makers as well as locals, with a weekly variety/cabaret show at the theatre called 'Songs from the Shows'. This showcased the different talents within the society, and also helped strengthen their relationship with The Playhouse.

In 2001, WOS presented the Weston amateur premier of 'Chess', which was applauded in the *Weston Mercury* for the impressive set and imaginative costumes, making it hard to believe it was an amateur production, and in autumn 2018, they took on the challenge of Andrew Lloyd Webber's 'Cats'. While some people may have felt this show to be too adventurous for an amateur society, WOS proved that nothing is too much for them as they delighted audiences with a combination of fantastic costumes, make-up and outstanding performances, achieving a nearly sold-out run over the five shows.

With the society always striving to entertain, they have provided audiences with

'The Mikado', 1985. Photograph courtesy of Weston Operatic Society.

'Chess', 2001. Photograph courtesy of Weston Operatic Society.

a high standard of entertainment over the years and their shows are always well supported. Welcomed with open arms, the society have always had a strong relationship with The Playhouse, which continues to grow.

While WODS may not have been around for quite as long as WOS, they too have a long association with The Playhouse, having made their debut in October 1984 with a production of 'Finian's Rainbow'. Performing at the theatre every year since, the society have consistently provided high entertainment value, with shows over the years including 'Oklahoma!', 'Kismet', 'Guys and Dolls', '42nd Street' and, more recently, 'Oliver!' and 'Priscilla Queen of the Desert'. President of WODS Tony Lay wrote to me as follows:

> WODS has always been a 'family' society, ever since six or seven families came together in 1972 to present a concert version of 'Oklahoma'; we even 'took it on tour', performing it at The Little Theatre in Wells. From then until 1983, we performed our shows at Worle Comprehensive School and our audiences built to the point that we felt we should 'spread our wings' and reach a larger and more central audience. Our first show at The Playhouse was 'Finian's Rainbow' in October 1984 which members of no less than 20 families took part in with late member Betty Nicholas taking on the role of director. WODS have always encouraged its members to take on production roles and they've done so for a vast majority of our shows since.

Following their debut in 1984, WODS have performed all of their main shows at The Playhouse, and in 2007, the longest-serving member of staff at the theatre, Pete Magor, was made Vice-President of the society, along with Dave Williams. Pete Tilke, Technical Facilities Manager at The Playhouse, also holds a role within the company since being made an honorary Vice-President in 2013.

Staff at The Playhouse have always been supportive of both societies, helping to come up with ideas for staging and encouraging the smooth running of shows. Both societies have been nominated for and won multiple awards since their formation, for set design and creative lighting as well as individual performers and stage management, and they continue to provide budding performers with the opportunity to perform on the stage.

'Finian's Rainbow', 1984.
Photograph courtesy of Worle Operatic Society.

'Me and My Girl', 2008.
Photograph courtesy of Worle Operatic Society.

'Oliver', 2017. Photograph courtesy of Worle Operatic Society.

The Friends of The Playhouse

On Tuesday 26th March 1991, The Friends of The Playhouse was formed to fill the gap left after the demise of the previous Theatre Club.

It all started when Alan Bowler, Entertainments Officer for Woodspring Council, put an advert in the local paper asking for expressions of interest to form a volunteer group to support the theatre. The aim of the organisation was to be the 'public face' of the theatre, to develop the image of the theatre as well as promoting it, to fundraise and to build a regular clientele. Members of The Friends would also benefit from discounts to shows, priority bookings and social functions.

An initial meeting was to be held at The Playhouse, but due to the overwhelming response, it was adjourned and relocated to the Winter Gardens. Over 100 people attended the meeting during which a constitution was put together, a committee was formed and 130 people signed up to become 'Friends'. Alan Bowler was quoted as saying that he was 'totally surprised' at the support from the public, which had exceeded all expectations, and that 'this can only do a lot of good for The Playhouse'. While the committee was set up to administer the activities of the group, it would have no say in management decisions within the theatre. A list of voluntary duties was also put together, which included the taking of tickets during shows, envelope stuffing and providing hospitality to performers back stage.

The first meeting of the committee was held on 18th April 1991, and it was announced that the first event to be held by The Friends would be a coffee morning on Saturday 27th April – this proved so popular that coffee mornings still take place today.

The Friends' logo

The initial fundraising by The Friends was through their membership fee. This was then followed by bucket collections after shows to raise much-needed funds for the theatre. Permission from the performers was always sought beforehand, and it was noted that collections were, and still are, always best during the pantomime season.

An open day in November 1991 organised by The Friends provided members of the public with the opportunity to go 'behind the scenes' of the theatre and learn what goes into putting on a show, as well as to find out about the history of the building. Taking up an idea pursued a few years before proved worthwhile as over 400 people attended and it was hailed a great success, with the membership of The Friends also receiving a boost. The open day has always proved popular with the public, and so The Friends have continued to host this event on an annual basis ever since.

*

With promotion and fundraising being the driving force behind The Friends, in 1992, they launched a 'Top Brass' seat sponsorship, which allowed businesses and individuals to sponsor a seat within the theatre. With businesses charged £50 and individuals £25, this idea proved popular, and it was repeated again in 1995. Although the sponsorship plaques are no longer fixed to individual seats, having been removed when all the seats were replaced in 2004, they remain part of the history of the theatre and can be viewed mounted on a board in the bar area.

When plans to improve the theatre were announced in 1994, The Friends' support was strong and they helped to come up with the idea of having a Victorian theme throughout the front-of-house area, including mahogany wood to give the entrance an air of high quality, as well as mirrors to create the impression of greater space. These plans were on show during another open day (which over 100 people attended) and Ken Tapley, Chairman of The Friends at the time, was quoted as saying: 'The aim of the open day was to get people more involved with The Playhouse. Lots of people go to the theatre and enjoy a show, but they are totally unaware of what goes into the workings of a theatre.'

But while many fans of the theatre attended the open day in a show of support for The Playhouse, others continued to run the theatre down, with Ken Tapley saying: 'One of the problems in this town is that we are quick to knock what is a very vital asset. Many towns would give their right arm to have a theatre like this.'

The Friends also helped other improvements take place when they raised £6,500 to upgrade the dressing rooms, which had remained much the same as when they were built 25 years ago. Improvements included new carpets, lowered ceilings and new mirrors with make-up lights which would make it easier for performers to prepare for the stage. The dressing rooms were officially opened by the Chairman of the council's Marketing and Leisure Committee, Councillor Bob Thompson, on 27th November 1994 and were the first of many improvements The Friends were considering along with Woodspring District Council.

While this was a busy time for the theatre, it was also busy for The Friends as the membership rose to over 500 members for the first time, thanks to the new management team raising the profile of The Friends and also giving them more opportunities to become involved at the theatre.

*

The Friends' biggest fundraising effort came in January 1995 when they teamed up with the *Weston Mercury* to create 'The Weston Mercury's Playhouse appeal'. The aim of the campaign was to raise £50,000 to improve disabled facilities at the theatre, which were described as 'totally inadequate'

Official opening of the dressing rooms.

Plaque to mark the refurbishment and opening of the dressing rooms.
Author's photograph.

with the need for improvement being 'desperate'.

Alan Bowler, Theatre Manager at the time, said:

> At the moment we have an audio loop system for people hard of hearing and
> only two spaces for wheelchairs. We have to carry people up the stairs and
> there are no disabled toilet facilities. The appeal is very important because
> we encounter people with disabilities daily and on occasion we have to turn
> them away.

Editor of the *Mercury* Judi Kiesel showed her support for the campaign,
saying:

> This is such a worthwhile cause. The *Mercury* has been a staunch advocate
> of the thriving Playhouse in the past. We believe this appeal will help the
> disabled to enjoy the theatre in the town and ensure our theatre continues
> to prosper in the future.

The appeal was also backed by leading disabled rights campaigner Tim
Shapley OBE who, having lived in the town for four years, commented that
The Playhouse was one of the worst buildings for people with mobility
problems to negotiate. He told the *Mercury*: 'I think the appeal is a jolly good
thing. I went to see The Playhouse in 1991 and I came to the conclusion that
it was a very difficult building to crack.'

Disabled access to the venue was initially highlighted in 1981 following the
installation of the hearing loop system. The Royal Association for the
Disabled had been invited to assess the building after the council rejected
an idea of creating a disabled access entrance at the rear of the theatre, as it
was noted that this would make it more difficult for people to enter the
venue due to there being two staircases to get to the auditorium. It was also
noted that there were no disabled toilets at the theatre.

One of the first ideas of the campaign was seat sponsorship. Similar to the
previous seat sponsorship idea which took place in 1992, seats were available
for businesses, societies and individuals to sponsor, with Lord Jeffrey Archer
becoming the first sponsor of many. Other sponsors included the *Weston*

Sponsors' plaques.
Author's photographs.

Mercury itself, Jill Dando, department store Walker & Ling, Weston MP Sir Jerry Wiggin, Deborah Kerr, Sir John Gielgud and Sir Anthony Hopkins. The first amateur dramatic society to sponsor a seat was The Red Triangle Players, who had performed at the theatre since 1948.

By the end of January, over £4,000 had been raised for the appeal, and a variety show was planned to boost funds. 'Good clean family fun' was experienced at the charity night in March, which was headlined by ventriloquist Ray Alan and Lord Charles, performing alongside local talent including singers, dancers and an illusionist. A total of £1,200 was raised during the night, adding to the boost received over the previous Christmas period when a treasure chest had been filled with coins from theatre-goers attending the pantomime 'Peter Pan'.

As the appeal gained support, various fundraising activities and events took place, including volunteers from the theatre taking part in the Weston Lions Club's ninth swim marathon, life-size cut-outs of Marilyn Monroe and James Dean being auctioned off and a Battle of the Bands competition organised, with judges from the music industry giving their expert opinions. The winners of this competition – World Machine – were invited to perform at the Grand Charity Gala planned for later on in the year.

The public really got behind the appeal, and money flooded in from all angles. Having raised money for charity previously with strength and endurance exercises, Iron Man and former Firefighter Phil Haskins did his bit for the appeal when he invited people to join him on a run along the sea front. General Manager of The Playhouse Alan Bowler and Admin Assistant Annie Skeath combined weight loss and fundraising, losing two stone between them and putting sponsor money towards the campaign, while Weston's longest-running baton-twirling group, the Worleybirds Majorettes, provided entertainment when they performed at the Sovereign Centre and Italian Gardens in April. Ranging in age from 5 to 15-years old, the group helped the appeal reach a total of £14,000, with funds going towards new seats as well as automatic doors to help disabled patrons enter the theatre, refurbishment of the loop system, Braille signs and the ultimate fund to install the stairlift.

Support for the appeal was also given by Lord Charles Forte, one of the world's leading hoteliers at the time, who had helped his uncle serve ice cream in his Weston parlour during his youth. Not forgetting his time in the town, Lord Forte made a personal contribution to the appeal.

Many more fundraising efforts kept the money coming in, including raffles, sponsored walks, a mile of coins along the sea front and the donation of profits from one of Weston Operatic Society's 'Songs from the Shows' performances. A masked ball was also held at the Winter Gardens in the summer, attended by the cast of the upcoming pantomime 'Cinderella' – including Jack Douglas from the 'Carry On' films and Jayne Collins from 'Baywatch'. The ball was ended at midnight in true Cinderella fashion.

A changeover of staff between the theatre and McDonalds also took place

Robbie Burns and Ken Dodd with a cheque towards the appeal.

to raise further funds. Swapping ushering duties for serving food and vice versa, staff from both venues enjoyed the experience and raised £100 in the process as McDonalds used money won in a marketing competition to sponsor a seat.

The Friends also came up with a unique way of raising money by giving away tubes of Smarties with the aim for people to fill them up, once empty, with five and 20 pence pieces, both of which fit snugly.

The appeal received a further boost when Betty and Adrian Harper, who had both performed at the theatre before the war, donated £200. With their association with the theatre dating back to 1936, Mr Harper said in support of the appeal 'We want to give something back to Weston for the happy years we spent on the local stage.'

*

While all efforts were being put towards fundraising to improve the facilities for the disabled, it was important for careful consideration to be made as to how best to improve the theatre to make a visit as easy and comfortable as possible for people with disabilities. In order to keep the process as open as possible, a disabled facilities forum was held at the theatre where an open discussion was planned about the new facilities. Representatives at the meeting included Woodspring District Council, the fire brigade, The Friends, a building surveyor and members of the public. It was hailed 'a valuable exercise' during which constructive comments were noted and included in the new plans.

As fundraising continued, Sunday 29th October 1995 marked the biggest event held for the appeal when the *Weston Mercury*, in association with The Playhouse Theatre presented a 'Night of Stars Grand Charity Gala Evening'. Introduced and compered by Lord Archer, the night boasted performances from local talent such as the Tina Counsell School of Dancing and Playhouse Youth Theatre group, as well as familiar names including Jimmy Cricket and The Barron Knights – all of whom gave their time for free.

Max Bygraves was due to close the show, but unfortunately due to illness was unable to perform. However, his absence didn't dampen the spirits of the audience who, during the mini celebrity auction, raised £500 for the appeal. Items up for grabs included a signed golf glove from Nick Faldo, signed photos from George Formby, John Major, Frank Bruno, Cliff Richard and Dolly Parton, as well as a signed menu by Michael Caine from his London restaurant Langan's. The evening raised £8,000 for the appeal, bringing the running total to £33,000, and was deemed a great success by all those who attended. Chairman of The Friends Ken Tapley agreed, telling the *Weston Mercury*: 'I am delighted. I think it is really wonderful now we can see the target in sight. The people of Weston should be congratulated for their generosity.'

With public support behind the appeal and appetites whetted for celebrity memorabilia, another auction was held on 18th November which contributed to the funds already raised.

Bringing the year of fundraising to a close, 'The Joy of Christmas' was held at The Playhouse on 17th December with all profits going towards the appeal.

Performers including The Paddy Payne Dancers and singers from Weston College and readings from both Weston Operatic Society and The Red Triangle Players, among others, provided seasonal entertainment before the traditional pantomime and helped to raise over £1,000 towards the appeal.

Thanks to a combination of efforts from local people as well as celebrities and The Friends, a huge number of events were staged throughout the year, bringing the total funds from the appeal to a healthy £43,000. Everyone was delighted with the efforts and the money raised, with Ken Tapley commenting:

> I would like to say thank you to everyone who helped. I am so impressed with the generosity of the people of Weston who have given so much to the appeal. It is also quite something when world-famous celebrities like Sir Anthony Hopkins and Deborah Kerr are interested enough to get involved.

It was hoped that donations that continued to flood in over the Christmas period would help them reach the target by early January 1996.

*

Thanks to the generosity and efforts of everyone involved, facilities for disabled patrons were able to be improved at the theatre and a stairlift was finally installed. It was unveiled by stars of the pantomime, actress Sophie Lawrence (Diane Butcher in 'EastEnders') and Bucks Fizz singer Mike Nolan in November 1997. Tim Shapley OBE, disability consultant and one of the main advisors who worked with the theatre when it installed the lift, said:

> Having this lift will make a big difference to myself and other disabled theatre-goers. I have wanted to come to The Playhouse many times over the last seven years I have lived in Weston, but have been unable to because I could not manage the stairs. Now I will be here at least once a month and have already attended one show which I enjoyed. I will tell all my friends as well.

Regular theatre-goer Geoff Bailey was also delighted with the changes to the theatre as the stairlift made his visits a more pleasant experience. Previously he had had to be carried up the stairs by three members of staff, but with the installation of the lift, he had a safe ride to the raised seating which gave

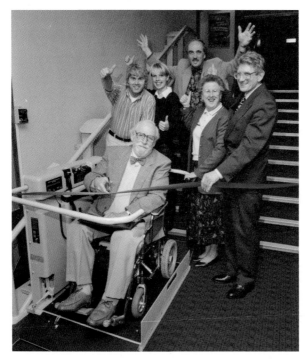

Unveiling of the new stairlift.

him a better view. Geoff said at the time:

> It is a very welcoming atmosphere. We went to see 'High Society' this week and heard at least three people say it was their first ever visit to The Playhouse because of the new access. A lot of people were put off by the indignity of being carried up the stairs, but because my wife Barbara and I really wanted to see the shows, I put up with that.

*

Following the successful fundraising year of 1995, the efforts of The Friends have continued up to this day, with the total money they've raised nearing £250,000. Over the years they have helped the theatre to continue to improve its facilities, including: an infra-red hearing loop system which was introduced in 1996; a new lighting control panel costing more than £7,000; and 20 new sets of headphones for the hard of hearing, as well as an £800 gauze

Unveiling of the new curtains.

curtain for the stage. Extra curtains – used to block off parts of the stage from the audience during performances – were also supplied by The Friends in 1999 and were unveiled by patron Ken Dodd before he entertained a sell-out audience with five hours of non-stop comedy.

*

In 2001 The Friends launched the Grand Piano appeal, for which they raised £10,000. The aim of the appeal was to raise enough money to buy a grand piano which could be permanently situated at the theatre. Up until that point, a piano was shared with the Winter Gardens and therefore every time each venue wanted to use it, it had to be moved and consequently retuned, costing quite a lot of money. Thankfully, the appeal proved successful and enough money was raised to buy a piano exclusively for the theatre which is still used to this day.

The 'Friendliest Theatre' trophy. Author's photograph.

*

Many of the improvements to the theatre couldn't have been completed over the years without the support of The Friends. While they have continued to hold social days out, Saturday coffee mornings, annual open day tours of the theatre, and to perform volunteer duties, they have also found the time to continue to fundraise, providing the theatre with invaluable support. Items which people may not realise have come from The Friends' fundraising include radios, stage lights, follow spots, baby-changing facilities and a PA system – items which the theatre couldn't do without.

In July 2009, The Friends also played their part in hosting an evening of entertainment to celebrate the 40th anniversary of the re-opening of the theatre, raising £500 in the process, which was put towards a new digital lighting desk. Front-of-House Manager Barry North praised The Friends for their support, saying: 'Without The Friends, quite frankly, I don't think we would have a theatre. Not only do they raise money, but they are an integral and vital part of the theatre's very being.' At this time the theatre was also presented with a trophy for 'Friendliest Theatre' by the Arts Council of the West of England, which is kept on top of the seat sponsorship board

Chandelier donated by The Friends to
celebrate 40 years of the new theatre.
Author's photograph.

in the bar area of the theatre.

As part of the milestone celebration, The Friends also donated a chandelier
which still takes pride of place above the staircase leading up to the circle
and continues to mesmerise audience members with its variety of colours.

With their fundraising efforts over the years, The Friends have helped the
theatre in many ways, and in 2015 they sponsored the first apprentice at the
theatre. This proved a success, with the member of staff continuing to work
at the theatre when the apprenticeship came to an end, and was a learning
point for other theatres in the country who now also employ apprentices,

Cast of 'Snow White and the Seven Dwarfs', 2016. Photograph courtesy of Neil Gibson.

Cast of 'A Story for All Time', 2017. Photograph courtesy of Sue Ball.

Cast and crew of 'Hercules', 2018. Photograph courtesy of Tim Moore.

giving people a much-needed boost in starting a career in the theatre.

More recently, The Friends have become a fixture in the programme of shows at the theatre with the creation of their own pantomime. Starting in 2016 with 'Snow White and the Seven Dwarfs', written and directed by Wendy Summers, the pantomime was a joint effort between members of The Friends and theatre staff, and provided a laugh a minute for the audience. Spurred on by the success of the show, Wendy wrote a second pantomime, 'A Story for All Time' based on 'Beauty and the Beast', which was performed in 2017 and was equally successful.

The story of 'Hercules', written by members of the front-of-house team, was the next pantomime to be performed in the summer of 2018, and it's hoped that The Friends' pantomime will continue as long as the traditional annual pantomime at the theatre.

*

The Friends have provided The Playhouse with many years of invaluable support. Their fundraising efforts have enabled the theatre to develop, upgrade and expand in many ways, and long may it continue.

Their hospitality has also been noted by many of the performers, including their late patron, Sir Ken Dodd, who told me 'The Friends have done a wonderful job over the years', and this was formally recognised when the theatre was voted the most hospitable theatre in England in 2003, winning the 'One-for-the-Pot' award. The theatre was the top choice among show promoters, who visit many theatres during their tours, and the award recognised the work of the theatre staff as well as The Friends. The award was a shiny kettle and teabags, which were no doubt used up quickly by the hard-working backstage crew.

Having spent time with members of the group, as well as working alongside them in my role as Box Office Assistant, I can feel their enthusiasm for the theatre and their desire to provide people attending the theatre with the best experience they can give. Their fundraising efforts continue to support the theatre to this day and without them, The Playhouse wouldn't be the same.

Sir Ken Dodd OBE

Born on 8th November 1927 in Knotty Ash, Liverpool, Kenneth Arthur Dodd OBE was the son of a coal miner.

Up until his death at the age of 90, Ken lived in the farmhouse he was born in, and showed no sign of slowing down despite his advancing years – but with the ability still to pull in a crowd and sell out shows, why wouldn't he carry on doing what he loved?

I wrote to Ken, as patron of The Friends of The Playhouse and a performer who had appeared there many times, firstly to congratulate him on his well-deserved knighthood, but also to ask him about his experiences of performing at The Playhouse. I received a very nice letter back in which he told me that he had 'played the lovely Playhouse many times over the years – nearly every year for at least the last twenty-five', but couldn't recall the date of his first performance. In response to my question about why he always returned, he wrote:

> I have always enjoyed my visits to this wonderful venue. The staff are so very helpful – backstage and front of house are always extremely welcoming. I am very pleased to say I have always played to full houses, which shows that you have wonderful support from locals as well as holiday makers. In fact, I receive letters from holiday makers who write that they couldn't get in because it was filled up by all the local supporters!

Ken accepted the offer to become patron of The Friends in July 1999. Presented with the patronage and honorary life membership of The Friends by Chairman John Ball, he said of the honour: 'The Friends of The Playhouse are quite amazing. This is truly the best team of Friends I have seen in the country. It is a pleasure to come and entertain here and I am greatly honoured to become a patron of this wonderful theatre.' Praising the efforts of The Friends, he also said: 'Theatre has to be a place where people love what they do. The Friends are a group of lovely people who want The Playhouse to be successful and to protect this vibrant hub of the town's cultural life.'

The Friends were equally as pleased to have Ken on board, and John Ball shared their excitement, saying:

Sir Ken Dodd.

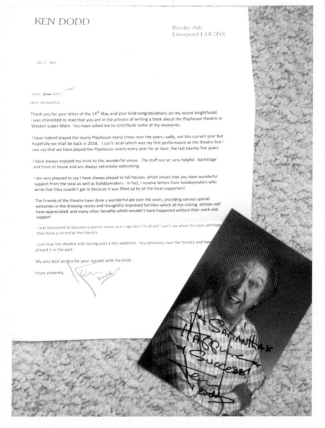

Sir Ken Dodd's letter to me, as well as a signed photograph. Author's photograph.

We are absolutely delighted that such a respected showman has decided to put his name to our organisation; when I announced it to the rest of The Friends you could see the look of amazement and joy in their eyes. We are proud to have him on board.

Ken also praised them in his letter to me, saying:

The Friends have done a wonderful job over the years, providing various special welcomes in the dressing rooms and thoughtful improved facilities which all the visiting artistes will have appreciated and many other benefits which wouldn't have happened without their work and support.

He finished his letter to me admitting that he 'just loves live theatre and slaving over a hot audience', which he continued to do until he sadly passed away after a short illness on 11th March 2018.

As a legendary performer who not only sold millions of records worldwide as a singer, but had the ability to keep an audience laughing way beyond his shows' finishing time, Ken will always be remembered at the theatre. In 2018, in tribute to him, The Friends commissioned and unveiled a plaque to honour his memory, ensuring that his timeless humour and performances at The Playhouse over the years will never be forgotten.

At the end of 2018, it was announced that Richard Cadell (Sooty's puppeteer) and Trevor Payne (from the successful and long-running variety show 'That'll be the Day') had accepted shared patronage of The Friends, taking over from Sir Ken Dodd.

Sir Ken Dodd's memorial plaque.
Author's photograph.

Panto at The Playhouse

Many people's first experience of live theatre is attending a pantomime and there really is something magical about seeing pantomime performed as an escape into a fantasy world for a couple of hours. With men and women playing opposite roles and audience participation, it's been a staple in theatres for many years and I'm sure everyone will have a special memory related to watching one.

For me personally, working front-of-house at the theatre, it's exciting to watch an audience arrive for a pantomime, as you can see the anticipation on the children's faces as well as the excitement from adults who are looking forward to sharing a fun time with their family and friends.

Although the Knightstone Theatre started hosting pantomimes before The Playhouse was created, the first pantomime to be held at The Playhouse was 'Babes in the Wood' in 1948. Unfortunately, following this debut, pantomime disappeared from the theatre until making a welcome return in 1957 with an amateur production of 'Sleeping Beauty'. However, by Christmas 1958, it was decided that there would be no pantomime in the town that year, but thankfully, to the joy of audience members, it came back to The Playhouse in December 1963 and has remained an annual tradition ever since – apart, obviously, from 1964-68 when the theatre was unusable following the fire.

The Playhouse has had a successful history of staging pantomimes, and it was noted in early 1964, following the 'Grand Family Panto' of 'Robinson Crusoe', that during its two-and-a-half-week run, it had been seen by over 11,500 people. Staged by Bunny Baron Productions, who went on to produce The Playhouse pantomime for many years, the show opened on Boxing Day – as was the tradition then – and full houses became the norm as coach

Stagehands for pantomime 'Cinderella', 1975.

parties from surrounding areas as well as local residents attended, with it being reported by the Deputy Entertainments Manager for the town as being 'the most successful panto we've ever had'.

The success of pantomime continued in the following years with advance bookings making up a lot of the profits, and new patrons being drawn to the theatre after hearing of the town's reputation for putting on a traditional pantomime. Audience figures were reported as being nearly 30,000 following a run of 4 to 6 weeks, and in 1976 'Cinderella' beat all previous attendance records at the theatre. Jack Martin, Woodspring Entertainments Manager at the time, was reported as saying: 'It has been the best pantomime of all time. We are delighted at how well it has done. The records for advance bookings and takings at the door have all been easily broken.'

A lot of hard work goes into every show at the theatre, but panto is on a different level with so many things going on at the same time, and sometimes the show is performed up to three times a day! But no matter how much effort is put in to ensure the show runs smoothly, sometimes mishaps can't be avoided, especially where the weather and nature are involved.

In 1979 a performance of 'Aladdin' had to be stopped due to heavy snow and a fear the audience might not be able to make it home, and in 1980 Cinderella's coach had to be pulled by only one real-life pony until a replacement could be found, as the other one had to be sent home for rest after showing signs of going into labour! Who would have thought that while families were being entertained in the auditorium, a vet was backstage predicting when a pony's labour was going to start! Despite the backstage drama, this particular run of 'Cinderella' held the record for attendances, even though the run was shorter than for previous shows – until the next year when records were broken again.

During the 1980s it was confirmed that the theatre's policy of putting on a traditional pantomime without the use of star names was proving successful as, year after year, advance bookings from people further and further afield showed that The Playhouse had something to offer. However, one panto, in particular, kept audiences waiting longer than normal when it appeared to

The cast of 'Cinderella', 1979.

rain inside the auditorium! The panto in question, 'Cinderella' in 1984, firmly remains in the memories of those involved as a funny event.

Former Technician Dave Gentle told me:

> During panto season in 1984 I was helping out as usual and was asked to take the safety curtain off. The problem was that there were two levers for this and two levers for the sprinklers – all of which were side by side and as soon as I pulled them, I realised what I'd done. As 100 gallons of water drenched the stage, it was clear I'd mixed them up, but all hands were on deck to clear the stage in time for the performance and it went ahead as normal – only 20 minutes later than planned!

House and Stage Manager Tony Blizzard praised everyone's efforts, saying: 'Everyone rallied round marvellously and with the firemen, they did a splendid job. They all set to with mops and buckets.' Paddy Payne also recalled this incident:

> When Dave nearly flooded the theatre it was the funniest thing ever. It was an easy mistake to make and suddenly it was raining inside! We had to try

and dry the curtains in time for the show, but occasionally during the performance you would get a drip come down from above, it was so funny. There was a scene with mops and the actors ended up mopping actual water! It was nice to know the system was effective if there had been a fire.

Pete Magor laughed at his memory of this, saying:

I think we held the performance off for only about half an hour, but the problem was that because the house curtains had gotten wet, during the performance an odd drip kept falling onto the stage – it was the water scene which hadn't made the cut!

Thankfully, the incident was quickly forgiven and, in true showbiz fashion, with everyone pulling together – including the cast, some of whom were already in their costumes – the show went ahead with no more hitches.

To mark the occasion and to also ensure he never forgets it, Dave was presented with his own award – 'The Gentle Touch' – a sprinkler on a wooden plinth with a plaque, which he has kept with pride!

'The Gentle Touch' award.
Photograph courtesy of Dave Gentle.

Panto brochures produced by Paddy Payne.
Author's photograph.

*

There were many years when the pantomime set box office records, with subsequent years tending to break the previous year's record, but in 1987 the future of the pantomime at the theatre was dealt a blow when BJB Productions (originally Bunny Baron's production company), which had produced the pantomime at the theatre for the past 17 years, closed down. The company had presented the first pantomime – 'Sleeping Beauty' – at the rebuilt theatre in 1969, but it was now time for a change. Finishing their association at the theatre with the same panto they started with, it was noted that over 10,000 people attended to see the production of 'Sleeping Beauty' in 1986, and it was estimated that by the end of the run in January 1987, nearly 17,000 people would have seen it.

Tenders from many companies offering to put on future pantos came in 'fast and furious', and Mr Jack Martin said at the time that he was 'confident of maintaining a traditional panto of the same length and of at least equal standard'.

The company which did take over the production of the pantomime was PJ Productions, headed up by Paddy Payne, who had previously been involved with dance shows at The Playhouse, taking on roles such as chaperone or choreographer, and her sister Julie. Already having a relationship with the theatre was a great advantage, and PJ Productions would go on to produce the pantomime for the next four years. Starting with 'Mother Goose', which was being performed in Weston for the first time, they got off to a good start, with advance bookings already over 1,000 by July 1987 – a huge increase on the previous year. The demand for tickets was a pleasant surprise to everyone, but the increased involvement of local people and theatre staff in the staging of the show breathed new life into the pantomime.

In the early 1990s, however, well-known faces were starting to enter the world of panto, and at The Playhouse it was no different. From TV stars to comedians and even 'Gladiators', The Playhouse has seen a variety of stars spending their Christmas in Weston to grace the stage as a star of the pantomime.

Panto posters.
Author's photograph.

Pantos at The Playhouse, 1948-49 to 2018-19

1948-49   'Babes in the Wood'

1949-50   No panto, a fairy play with music 'The Beggar Prince' by Cicely Hamilton

1950-51   No panto as the theatre was closed, as was the Knightstone

1951-52   No panto as the theatre was closed

1952-53   No panto – winter rep experiment, with the Unicorn Players presenting 'A Party for Christmas' by C. Hunter

1953-54   Local bookings only

1954-55   No panto as the theatre was closed

1955-56   No panto as the theatre was closed

1956-57   No panto as the theatre was closed

1957   'Sleeping Beauty' performed 4th to 11th January by an amateur club

1958-59   No panto

1959-60   No panto

1960-61   No panto

1961-62   No panto

1962-63   No panto

1963-64   'Grand Family Panto', 'Robinson Crusoe'

1964-69   Theatre was closed due to the fire

1969-70   'Sleeping Beauty'

1970-71   'Robinson Crusoe'

1971-72   'Cinderella'

1972-73   'Aladdin'

1973-74   'Puss in Boots'

1974-75   'Jack and the Beanstalk'

1975-76   'Cinderella'

1976-77   'Sleeping Beauty'

1977-78   'Dick Whittington and his Cat'

1978-79   'Aladdin and his Wonderful Lamp'

1979-80   'Cinderella'

1980-81   'Sleeping Beauty' (Len Howe and Des King)

1981-82   'Jack and the Beanstalk'

1982-83   'Little Red Riding Hood'

1983-84   'Aladdin and his Wonderful Lamp'

1984-85   'Cinderella'

1985-86   'Dick Whittington and his Cat'

1986-87   'Sleeping Beauty'

1987-88   'Mother Goose'

'Puss in Boots', 1973.

'Aladdin', 1983.

1988-89 'Babes in the Wood'
1989-90 'Aladdin'
1990-91 'Robinson Crusoe'
1991-92 'Cinderella' (Barry McGuigan)
1992-93 'Snow White' (Ted Rogers from '321')
1993-94 'Aladdin' (Jenny Powell)
1994-95 'Peter Pan' (Melissa Bell from 'Neighbours')
1995-96 'Cinderella' (Jayne Collins, from 'Baywatch', Felice Arena from 'Neighbours' and Jack Douglas from 'Carry On' films)
1996-97 'Jack and the Beanstalk' (Keith Harris & Orville & Cuddles, and Arthur Bostram from 'Allo 'Allo)
1997-98 'Dick Whittington' (Sophie Lawrence, from 'Eastenders', Mike Nolan from Bucks Fizz and a special appearance by Budgie the Helicopter)
1998-99 'Aladdin' (Stefan Dennis from 'Neighbours' and Rocket from 'Gladiators')
1999-00 'Snow White and the Seven Dwarfs' (Anne Charleston)
2000-01 'Cinderella' (Adele Silva and Jack Douglas from 'Carry On' films)
2001-02 'Jack and The Beanstalk' (Antonio Fargas)
2002-03 'Peter Pan' (Derek Griffiths and Sonia)
2003-04 'Aladdin' (Peter Amory and John Pickard)
2004-05 'Snow White and the Seven Dwarfs' (Bernie Clifton, Kim Hartman and Danielle Nicholls)
2005-06 'Cinderella' (Jimmy Cricket)
2006-07 'Dick Whittington' (Shaun Williamson)
2007-08 'Jack and the Beanstalk' (Bruce Jones, and Sue Hodge from 'Allo 'Allo)
2008-09 'Peter Pan' (Timmy Mallet, and David Griffin from 'Hi De Hi' and 'Keeping up Appearances')
2009-10 'Snow White' (Vicki Michelle from "Allo 'Allo and Peter Duncan from 'Blue Peter')
2010-11 'Cinderella' (Sean Wilson from 'Coronation Street', Kelle Bryan from Eternal and John Lyons from 'A Touch of Frost')
2011-12 'Aladdin' (John Challis)
2012-13 'Sleeping Beauty' (Lorraine Chase and Same Difference from 'X Factor')
2013-14 'Jack and The Beanstalk' (George Sampson)
2014-15 'Peter Pan' (Dean Gaffney and Gemma Bissex)
2015-16 'Cinderella' (Joe Swash)
2016-17 'Beauty and the Beast' (John Challis)
2017-18 'Aladdin' (John Altman)
2018-19 'Snow White and the Seven Dwarfs' (Linda Lusardi)

Behind the Scenes

Everyone knows that a theatre is more than a building; it's a community with numerous people working together, both in front of and behind the scenes, to ensure a smooth running. When you attend the theatre, you will see box office assistants, bar staff, kiosk staff and ushers, but there are many others working hard whom you may never see, but whose roles are vitally important to the running of the theatre.

As well as researching and learning about the history of The Playhouse, I went behind the scenes to get to know the people whom you may never see, but without whose roles the show can't go on.

The longest-serving member of the team is Pete Magor who, having worked at The Playhouse on and off since the 1960s, has a wealth of knowledge about the theatre. As we got comfortable in our seats at the back of the auditorium, my first question to Pete was about how he got involved with The Playhouse. He told me:

> I knew the Stage Manager and he wanted people that knew how to operate a theatre, so rather than advertise, three of us transferred from the Knight-stone Theatre and for a time we were running both theatres.

Starting at the theatre as Chief Electrician, Pete was in fact the only electrician at the time, and also took on the role of lighting design, lighting his 1,000th show in 1991 during a performance of 'Weston Our Weston', although he admitted he stopped counting a while ago!

Naturally, during his time at the theatre, Pete has met many performers, and I was keen to find out if anyone stood out for him. He told me 'Brian Rix

'Weston Our Weston', 1991.
Photograph courtesy of Sharon Poole.

was the first person I met here. He performed the first six weeks of 'Let Sleeping Wives Lie' before Leslie Crowther took over, although they didn't perform the same part.' Pete also told me about meeting Cilla Black: 'When she was setting up there were two stools on the stage and she invited me to sit and chat with her, which I did.' When I asked if she was as nice as she seemed on TV, Pete confirmed this, saying: 'Yes, she was. I find that most people relate to theatre people and they're ok. Performers know they have to work alongside you and they appreciate what you do. There were a few awkward ones, but I can't mention names!'

Ken Dodd also stuck out in Pete's memories: 'He used to come here quite regularly, about two or three times a year – and that's how I got to know him – I got to know him pretty well.' When recalling a time Ken arrived to perform, Pete told me:

I remember one day he came in and I asked him if he was going to be doing a mic check and he joked 'Young man, if you don't know what I want now, you never will!' That was only once, as he always did a sound check, but that was the thing about Ken, he always had time for people.

A memory of Jimmy Cricket also made Pete laugh:

> He did a summer season here splitting his time between us and Weymouth. One time he had this idea of a Mexican hat dance, with every time he came on stage he would be wearing a bigger hat. One day he came in his van, which had only one hat in it, but we only just got it in the scene dock as it was huge! He used it once or twice here, but then realised it wasn't practical any more. We had to wheel it onto the stage it was so big – it must have cost him a bit!

While meeting the performers and having a joke with them can be fun, sometimes getting ready for a show can prove a challenge, as Pete recalled having to repair the theatre a couple times following incidents:

> During the Houdini musical in 2007, we had to fill up a water tank which weighed two tonnes and when we did, it went straight through the floor! We had to take the ceiling down underneath to repair the floor and then had to buy in boards to put the frame on – it was a horrendous job. We also had 'A Midsummer Night's Dream' here which had a hollow tree centre stage and when we did the get-out following the show, it fell over with one of the branches going straight through a wall!

As well as his involvement with helping to install sets and set up for shows, Pete's knowledge of electrics was applauded when the infra-red burglar alarm he installed in early 1991, following a previous burglary, alerted the police to a second attempt. He told me:

> Someone got in through the roof and came down a rope onto the stage. They managed to get into the control box and took out the rack with all the equipment in, including a CD player and effects unit, and made it to the stage door, but they then left the equipment at the top of the steps as they went out the stage door not realising that it closes behind you and you can't open it from the outside, so the equipment was still there when the police arrived!

After so many years of working at The Playhouse, Pete has seen many changes, and while he may now work more on a casual basis, there's something that keeps him there. I was intrigued to find out what it might be, but he told me he can't leave as 'they won't let me go due to my knowledge of both the theatre and electrics!'

*

Someone else who has spent many years at The Playhouse, but hasn't yet topped Pete's record of over 50 years, is Dave Gentle. Dave became 'official' on The Playhouse books when he was only 16 years old, in the early 1980s, having helped out for a couple of years before this, and was taken under the wing of General Manager Tony Blizzard and Pete Magor, who trained him to do lights, sound, follow spot and film projection, starting him on a career path which he told me he 'kind of fell into'. At one point, Dave was the youngest film projector in the country, screening films – including those marked '18' – at the tender age of 16.

Dave's first full-time role at the theatre was as a theatre assistant, starting on 1st April 1985. This included assisting both the front-of-house management as well as back stage, and his skills were further developed when he combined this with carpentry and electrics training, which he put to good use when he worked on a production of 'Joseph and the Amazing Technicolor Dreamcoat'. Over the years, Dave's role developed and his last position at The Playhouse was Technician and Stage Manager before he left the world of full-time theatre in 2017, although he admitted he considered himself more of a Technician than a Stage Manager, having spent years perfecting his craft involving lighting, sound and carpentry.

While I may have some knowledge of theatre, I decided to find out more, and asked Dave what these roles actually involve. Dave explained:

> The Stage Manager is ultimately responsible for everything which takes place on stage, and it's their role to ensure things are done safely and shows run smoothly with every aspect fitting together. This could include setting up the flying of scenery if needed in a production, and also the safe storage of props. It's the role of the Stage Manager and Technicians to work closely

The green room.
Author's photographs.

together along with the backstage crew to turn a bare stage into one fit for an audience – this is what is known as the 'get-in' and involves bringing the equipment into the theatre, setting up lights, sound and plotting scenery. As every show or performer's requirements are different, working with the company Stage Manager (if there is one) is crucial, and a lot of hard work and effort is put into setting everything up well before the audience arrives.

So, how did Dave become involved with the theatre? With his mum having worked in the box office and his sisters as usherettes, The Playhouse could be seen as a family business for the Gentle family – especially as Dave's son also works there – but it was visiting the theatre at a young age to watch the variety shows during the summer season that really sold it to him. He told me:

> All I've ever known is theatre and I don't know of anything else. I grew up seeing my mum go to work at the theatre and became fascinated by it. When we went to pick her up, if she wasn't quite finished, I would stand at the back of the auditorium and watch the performance. I became fascinated by famous people.

This fascination with famous people started Dave's passion for autograph collecting, a passion I also share, so it was fitting that when we met up, we sat in the green room of the theatre which is decorated ceiling to floor with signed pictures of the many performers who have graced The Playhouse stage over the years. Surrounded by hundreds of stars, this room holds a certain magic as it shows the variety of performers who have spent time at the theatre, from TV stars to comedians, and while some of them may no longer be with us, there will always be a reminder of their presence at the theatre. This room is also a favourite on the theatre tours held by The Friends.

Talking of famous people, Dave was happy to tell me about performers who have stood out in his memory, and he had quite a few to choose from:

> The biggest impression anyone made on me was Nigel Kennedy. It was an absolute privilege to see him as he is a master of his trade and was world class. Alan Carr was very friendly, and Norman Wisdom made a lasting impression as one of the nicest people I've met. Bobby Davro was a bit of a sore loser when it came to playing table tennis backstage, but he took it in good humour. Gary Wilmot also sticks in my mind as he was very down to

earth and arrived at the theatre driving the tour bus himself!

While Dave now holds a more casual role at the theatre, The Playhouse remains in his heart, as when we neared the end of our chat, he told me: 'I came into the theatre for the interest, but theatre is also in my blood.'

*

I also met with another former Technician Dave Clothier during a Friends' coffee morning and I could tell he had really put some thought into recollecting his memories of working at The Playhouse when he produced a few notes he'd written down. Retiring in 2008 after working full time at the theatre for 17 years, Dave told me that he couldn't remember much, but soon found his rhythm and had many stories to tell.

Having worked at the Knightstone Theatre before The Playhouse, Dave's involvement with the theatre started when his mother, who was a member of The Wayfarers, asked him to help produce seven versions of a painting for their latest production. After producing the props, the Stage Manager asked him if he wanted to help out for the week, and he then gained a role at The Playhouse working the follow spot and helping backstage if needed. After helping out with maintenance on a casual basis, Dave soon became a permanent member of the backstage crew.

Looking back at his time working at The Playhouse, Dave laughed when he told me:

> I remember Jimmy Cricket performing a summer season at the theatre, and during his show, the dancers on stage were doing Irish dancing. Jimmy came on from up stage and as he made his way to the front of the stage, dancing along with the girls, cloths were flying in as he approached, meaning that the stage was getting narrower and narrower. As part of the gag he got hit by a dancer, so went off and came back with a leg cast, and then continued to go on and off stage, each time gaining another cast, such as one for his arm, and he then had a bandage around his head, meaning he ended up looking like a mummy! His son Frankie and I had him on a stretcher by the end of

the gag. It was a fun season to work on.

Dave also recalled the time when he locked the star of the pantomime in the theatre:

Kim Hartman from 'Allo 'Allo!' came here to do panto as the Wicked Queen in 'Snow White' and I ended up locking her in – accidentally of course. At the end of the evening, I went round to lock up the theatre and called out to see if anyone was still there. I checked the dressing rooms and, as no one was around, I then left. We used to all drink in a pub near the theatre, so I was sitting there with the Company Stage Manager one night when he got a call from Kim to say she was in darkness at The Playhouse. I rushed straight over with him and as soon as I unlocked the stage door, she burst out, causing me to go flying. She obviously wasn't very happy and said she'd been in the shower so hadn't heard me calling out. I got her a big bouquet of flowers the next day to say sorry, and after that we got on well. However, she got her revenge on me during the last night of panto when she walked laughing off stage with a custard pie and threw it straight in my face!

Everyone who has worked with Ken Dodd has a special memory of him, and Dave is no different, telling me that he spent time on stage with the late comedian:

Anne, Ken's partner (who later became his wife), told me once that their stooge was away and asked if I would help him out with his act. She told me all I had to do was walk onto the stage casually and take his red furry coat from him. I thought 'that sounds easy' so agreed to do it. I walked onto the stage when I was told to and he asked me why I was there. I told him that I was there to take his coat, and he said 'Oh, you've given yourself words now, have you?' He then gave me his coat and asked me to put it on along with his hat which I did, and then as I turned to leave the stage, he asked me where I was going. I told him and he joked that I'd given myself more words, saying that I was really building up my part, causing both us and the audience to laugh. I was only meant to walk on and off stage, but ended up being there for about 20 minutes getting hotter and hotter under the stage lights as I was standing there in the coat and hat!

Talking about his on-stage moment with Ken reminded Dave of another memory connected to him:

> I was doing follow spot with another member of the team when, all of a sudden, she slipped off the stool with the cable caught around her foot, which meant the follow spot went off Ken and ended up flying towards the top of the stage. Ken took it in good humour, telling the audience 'Oh, there's another usherette gone flying' as he made a joke about it. She apologised to him after the show and he ended up giving her a £5 tip! We got a tip from him every time he performed.

Ensuring shows run smoothly is all down to the collaboration of the various departments within the theatre and, although working backstage can be a strict environment, as the crew are ultimately responsible for ensuring everything goes as it should, Dave told me of the fun he had when he worked backstage, a time when the crew had to use their initiative to save getting into trouble, and also of his favourite moment:

> Everyone enjoys the fact that there is a deadline as the show has to go on, but we used to have fun during shows and would sometimes play cards during scene changes. We also used to help out with putting costumes in the wash for some productions, but once we accidentally shrunk a dress. To get it back to normal for the show we ended up stretching it out with stage weights so no one would know and thankfully it worked! My favourite moment at the theatre was when Sir David Frost appeared. He was doing 'An Evening With …' and wanted to show a projection on the stage using footage from VHS cassettes. We had to disconnect the player from the crew room as it was the only one we had, and also borrowed a video mixer from Weston Tech College to be able to put the footage together. We went through what he wanted to show, and I had to make a note of the time clips for each piece of footage, so I knew where to start and finish each bit. I was really nervous as I wanted to do my best for him to ensure the evening went smoothly, so was anxious throughout. He showed the interview with President Nixon, among others, and at the end he told me that this was the first time during his tour the projection footage had gone smoothly. It was a proud moment and also my favourite.

As Dave shared various funny moments with me, one which sticks in his mind, but may remain in a few children's minds for another reason, involved Tchaikovsky's *1812 Overture*:

> I can't remember whether it was the Weston Town Band or the RAFA Band, but they asked if they could have the sound of cannons when they played the 1812 overture. We said 'yes' and wired it all up under the stage so we could set them off when needed. But after performing with the band, the St Mark's Choir sat down on the forestage for the piece of music to be played and sat right above where the thunderclaps were placed. We knew what was going to happen, but there wasn't anything we could do about it, so had to go ahead as planned, and laughed as all the kids jumped when the cannon noises went off. It was so funny to watch!

*

Having a true passion for the theatre is something that both Pete Tilke and Mark Thompson share.

Starting as a casual member of staff in 1998, Pete Tilke has had a varied career at The Playhouse and has worked his way up through many roles. From helping backstage to juggling both front-of-house and backstage duties, before becoming the Front-of-House Manager, and eventually graduating from Technical Apprentice to Technical Facilities Manager, he knows every aspect of what goes on in the theatre, and his passion for it shows. Wanting to be immersed in the environment of theatre from a young age, Pete told me that with theatre, you 'either love it or you hate it and there's a certain buzz about it and what you can achieve. That's what I love about it and every day is different which is quite exciting.'

Pete recalled honing his technical skills from a young age, putting on shows for his family during which he would play with the lights while his cousins would provide the music. Now, as Technical Facilities Manager, Pete is involved with every aspect of setting up for a show, including the lighting, sound and installation of the sets. Having never been tempted to perform on the stage – although he has been dragged on by both Ken Dodd and Bobby Davro – Pete's passion is for the technical side of the theatre. He told me:

Every day you come into the theatre and you've got an empty stage, completely blank, with nothing on it. You start setting up, so you unload a lorry and bring in all the flight cases and you fly in the scenery, put up lights, put the sound in and then you create a stage. You complete the sound checks and the lights and then you open the house to the public. They come in, sit down and watch the show, thoroughly enjoying it, and then they leave and you start taking everything down, load it back on the lorry and within 12–14 hours, you've created a show. That's what I think is the most enjoyable thing because you turn it around so quickly, and then the next day another lorry turns up with a different show, different requirements and a different audience. That's what I love, every aspect is different and no day is the same – you get a buzz from that.

Pete also talked about the variedness of the sets and stages that can be created: 'It's all an illusion and smoke and mirrors, and about what you can create in a real environment with no CGI or anything like that.' I mentioned that some sets don't change throughout a performance, such as the plays 'Judgement in Stone', which was performed in 2007, and 'The Shawshank Redemption' in 2016, but how, as an audience member, you are immersed in it, fully believing that the set is a house or some other location. Pete agreed, saying:

Yes, you are the fourth wall and you are immersed in that setting and what we do technically is try and enhance that environment, be it by lighting or sounds, and there's so many things you can do with lighting and sound to replicate real life. That's the joy of technical theatre as you are taking a real-life situation and replicating it on stage. We have to make theatre special, which we do.

While every effort is made to recreate real life on the stage, the sheer size of sets can prove a challenge, as The Playhouse found out when 'Blood Brothers' was performed. Pete told me: '"Blood Brothers" was a massive production with three articulated lorries full of sound and lighting. It was tight, but we made it happen.' Other sets have also proved a challenge, with Pete saying:

We're not the biggest venue, but we're not the smallest venue either, we're very much middle of the road and what we do here very much pushes the boundaries of what we can get on the stage and with 'Blood Brothers' and 'Joseph' we were probably working towards the top end of our size and scale. It was a tough job, but thoroughly worth doing. That's what gets me out of bed each morning.

As well as the buzz of creating a stage, over the years Pete has met quite a few stars, with a couple standing out for him: 'My personal one was Lee Evans. I really enjoyed him because he was so down to earth, so warm and chatty and there was no starry celebrity about him, he was so unassuming.' Someone else whom Pete had admiration for was Norman Wisdom:

He came and did 'An Evening With …', and it was the first show I ever did being side of the stage. The audience gave him a standing ovation as he walked out on stage and it was just such a genuinely lovely feeling that the people who came to see him really did love him and what he did. When he came off into the wings at the end, he looked at the clock and asked 'How long have I been on?' and after I told him he then said 'Would you mind if I just ran back across the stage?' I told him he could do what he felt he needed to do, and so he just ran along the back of the stage in front of the audience and into the wings on the other side! He looked as if he was really tired when he came off, but doing that looked as if it gave him a boost and he thanked us all for what we did and he was great to have in the building. That was a memorable time.

When meeting performers, you can't help but think you know what they will be like, but Pete smiled when he told me: 'It makes me smile when you get a real A1 celebrity and they come to the stage door and feel they need to introduce themselves, and it's like, we do know who you are!' That shows that many performers are down to earth and when I asked if anyone stuck in his mind, Pete told me: 'Russell Brand sticks out like that as he came to the stage door and introduced himself, then went on stage, did his thing and left. He kept himself to himself.' Roy Chubby Brown was also different in real life to how he is on stage, with Pete saying: 'Roy Chubby Brown is known as being really crude on stage, but off stage he's a completely different gentleman. He's a nice bloke.'

Pete's passion for the theatre showed through when he told me:

> Someone did a radio interview once about theatre and they said 'Theatre is a group thing. It's something where everyone comes together. There is no hierarchy, there is no them and us. Basically the performers on stage cannot do what they do on the stage without the support and technical people behind them, but it also works both ways, as the technical people working backstage can't do what they do without the artist on stage, so there has to be that mutual respect.' I think it's testament to a good theatre when there is respect for the different areas.

This proved true with several of the performers Pete recalled:

> Ken Dodd would always remember you. When I was there to welcome him on stage, he would know me by name and say: 'Oh you've been here for some time'. Joe Pasquale will always remember you as well. It means something to me when they know and remember you.

Pete also expressed his pride for the theatre and how, as time has gone on, The Playhouse is now firmly in the minds of performers:

> For me I am very proud of this venue. I am very proud of how it's kept, and some artists who come here take the time to say what a lovely kept venue it is. You want them to come again and when they're planning a tour in the future to choose The Playhouse. We are very much on Bristol's doorstep, and I think they are very aware of what we are beginning to do and the productions we are beginning to stage are very much treading on their toes. We're now fighting for the same audience.

Although I felt I hardly needed to ask the following question, as Pete's passion for theatre was clear throughout our conversation, as with everyone I met up with, I wanted to find out what has kept him at The Playhouse for over 20 years. He told me:

> It's because every day is different. Something new always comes along, or Mark will book a production which I can't wait to be in the venue, or I think I can't wait to work on. Because we work up to 12 months in advance, we're

always working towards shows, and it's the big shows, now we've stepped into that field, that have kept me here. When Mark came, he changed the whole programme, which then refreshed it and I felt invigorated by all the new quality productions that have been coming and hopefully it will continue.

*

With Pete's impassioned views about The Playhouse in mind, I asked General Manager Mark Thompson if he agreed with this, and he did, saying:

> We are attracting much bigger content than the venue has done in the past. We sit in the front garden of the Bristol Hippodrome, and what they do they do well, as we're never going to do that scale of product as regularly, but I think that I've probably stepped on their toes more than they will ever step on mine, as I've accepted their position and it's a good healthy place to be.

Joining The Playhouse family as General Manager in January 2014, Mark's role at the start was very different to how it is now. Recalling his early days at the theatre, Mark told me:

> Originally, when I first started here, it was about mapping the theatre out and actually getting the theatre to a position where it could be sustainable, and getting the right people in the right positions, which I think I have done now. The role has now shifted slightly, with it being more of a mentor role to the senior staff and about leading them down what can sometimes be a difficult road. What's different in theatre compared to other professions is that we don't have a tomorrow – we are always working towards a deadline, and the show must go on.

As General Manager, Mark's role is to oversee and take responsibility for the whole theatre. He told me:

> I have full creative view on the programme each year and decide what will and won't work and, even though we have a second level of management in place, predominately the decisions and processes are led from me. It's about keeping the building running, and no two days are the same. If everything is running smoothly, then the theatre is doing its job.

As a former 'theatre child' who enjoyed performing as well as attending performances, Mark has always loved theatre, but I wanted to know what makes it exciting for him and, despite having the ability to book the shows that perform at the theatre, his answer isn't what you might think:

> I love the shows and the shows are the crux of theatre, but that's not it for me, it's the audience. It's the way they react, it's the way if you watch a child watch a live performance, they become mesmerised, or how someone could be in one mood, and that changes when they see a live show and it takes them somewhere else. Theatre is about escapism and about how you can leave your daily life outside and for one moment you can extend into something bigger. There is nothing more rewarding in theatre than standing in a packed auditorium and not looking at the stage, but looking at the audience. We get to create dreams and memories. People always remember their experiences in the theatre and that's a really privileged place to be and it actually makes all of that hard work worthwhile.

Naturally, at some point, most of the staff in the theatre will come into contact with the performers, and I asked Mark how involved he gets with them, as General Manager:

> I am very 'hands-on' with the performers, as I manage that relationship through from the initial conversation right until the end. I always try to say hello if I'm around, as I think it's important that they know they have a relationship with me, and a lot of the feedback that I've had over the years is that it's very unusual for the venue manager to come out of his way to say hello, but that's part of this venue and the makeup. To a certain extent, I'm the one who is out there to promote the theatre, and the little touches and conversations I've had set us apart as a small theatre. It's important people remember us. For example, one performer told me she likes Maltesers, so now whenever she comes here I make sure someone puts them in her dressing room, and whenever acts come a long way I make sure there's a card in their dressing room from the team to welcome them.

So, with The Playhouse no longer relying on the council subsidy it once did for many years, and having been in his role for over five years, I asked Mark if his ambitions for the theatre are different from what they were when he started. He told me:

> Yes, they are. It's not unfair to say that I inherited a venue that had perhaps lost its way a little bit. Despite the fact all the ingredients were here, it just needed a chef and perhaps it had become a bit complacent in its position and as a venue had stopped being ambitious. It hadn't really tried to push the boundaries for a number of years and had become a little stale in the overall feeling of the building and the shows it was attracting. I think with a fresh set of eyes from someone who didn't have a history with the building, I could look at it differently.

With his ambitions to bring in new, fresh and bigger shows, Mark acknowledged that it hasn't been an easy journey telling me:

> We've had to get Weston to re-engage with the building and find a way to drum up enough local interest so that people start looking at the building again. Introducing new shows is the easy part, but what's more challenging is keeping that standard up, because in a way you become a victim of your own success. With new audiences, thanks to the comedy and big musicals, hopefully those who have come on the journey with us have seen the changes and can see the benefit of them.

Since his arrival at The Playhouse, it's clear to see that Mark has wanted to push the theatre to its limits by attracting new audiences and bigger shows, and he has definitely achieved this. He acknowledged that there has been a shift at the theatre:

> Five years ago I was on the phone to promoters continually asking them to bring their product to us. … [Now, we] get offered content, and you look at the tour list and a lot of the time we are the smallest venue on the list, and that's something to be proud of. Our technical team is second to none, and The Friends have funded so much over the years. There are not many theatres of this scale which can match us in terms of technical ability. We are now a very strong venue.

Memories and Funny Stories

As well as researching and collecting facts, during the process of celebrating The Playhouse, I have spoken to people about their memories of the theatre, whether they have worked there, have volunteered as a Friend, have performed on stage or have simply enjoyed visiting the theatre over the years and have had many to choose from, although, unfortunately, I only have space to include a small selection here.

Ian Gibson, whose father performed on the stage, wrote down his memories of the theatre, which were kindly shared with me by his family.

He was born in 1938, at around the time his father moved his pharmacy business to number 2 High Street, where the box office of the theatre is now situated. The Market Hall was set back from the road, with the entrance in the position currently occupied by the back row of the stalls, and a green-grocer's shop stood where the stairlift is now located.

Ian's father founded The Wayfarers Drama Group in 1951, and in 1954 they made their debut on The Playhouse stage with a play called 'How Now Hecate', which proved a great success, doubling its takings each night.

In 1956, the theatre was closed for most of the winter, but The Wayfarers put on three shows, and during other years, if there was nothing on at the Knightstone Theatre, The Playhouse was opened for just one week so that the group could perform. While a member of staff from the Winter Gardens would act as manager, Rex Hughes, who looked after backstage, worked the lighting, and the group did all of the other jobs themselves, including staffing the box office.

Seat plaque in memory of Ian Gibson's father. Author's photograph.

Ian recalled the excitement of the box office opening for the first time during the run of a show: 'Dad and I would come downstairs from the flat and cross over to the box office and with a bit of luck there were a couple of people waiting. Later we would claim of course that there was a "queue" waiting for tickets!'

*

For a child interested in drama, having the opportunity to perform on a stage in a real theatre is a dream. When I caught up with Anthony Keyes, who has performed at The Playhouse theatre twice, he recalled his memories of appearing in the first play to be performed at the theatre about the history of Weston-super-Mare, 'Snow on the Shore'.

Performed between 27th November and 1st December 1973, 'Snow on the Shore' was written and directed by two members of the Weston Dramatic Society, Nona Hooper and Bill Clout, providing a 'whistle-stop trip through 73 years of the town', starting in 1900 and going up to the present day. Told through the eyes of three generations of the same family, the show had a cast of over 40, from children to adults, and over 200 costumes were made for the production.

With moments of both comedy and sadness, songs and dancing, the show informed the audience of the major events in the town's history, such as the opening of the Grand Pier (and its fire) and of the Winter Gardens, the impact of the two World Wars, and even the opening of The Playhouse Theatre itself.

Poster advertising 'Snow on the Shore'.
Author's photograph.

Anthony told me:

> I was 14 at the time and interested in drama, so when I took part in the
> production I made a note of things that were happening. When I was being
> made up by the make-up lady, I took an interest in what make-up she was
> using and asked questions. I wrote my notes in the dressing room while I
> was experiencing it and I can recall the songs from the show even now.

Reading through Anthony's account of performing in the show, it's fascinating to see how varied his notes are. For example, as well as the information
about the make-up – 'our eye lids are made pale and for our lips we have
stick no 8' – he also recounts technical details such as 'our dressing room
was on the top floor' and 'there is an intercom on all the dressing room walls
so that we know what is going on on the stage and when to come on'.

What's even more fascinating is how, as a young boy, Anthony picked up on
audience reactions: 'I did not know audiences could change so much each
night of the show, some nights they would clap and laugh at anything and
other nights you hardly heard a noise.'

One of Anthony's roles was as a young boy called Bobby, whose job it was
to announce the fire of the Grand Pier. He recalled: 'What I enjoyed about
performing in the show was that I could put into practice what I was learning. This show was the people of Weston telling the history of Weston.'

Praise and congratulations were lapped upon the cast of the show from the local press, including the *Bristol Evening Post* which praised 'the very high standard of acting'.

*

When I met with Paddy Payne, she told me how she has been associated with The Playhouse Theatre for as long as she could remember. As well as producing The Playhouse pantomime for four years in the late 1980s, she has also been involved in dance shows. She told me:

> I just absolutely adore the theatre – I have always loved it. I have seen different sides of it during my time, but I think my talents are in my feet. I once had to work the soundboard for one of my shows, and I did it ok, but it terrified me – I wouldn't ever want to do it again!

Paddy told me about how she once lived near the theatre when she was younger, about the layout of the old theatre and about how she became involved with dance:

> I lived opposite the original theatre and remember there were washtubs out the front where people would take their washing. As a child I knew it was there, but I didn't become involved with it until much later. The original theatre had sackcloths over the top (hessian drapes) and there were shops either side. It was such a small passageway you would go down to the theatre, and the stage was awful. I remember the layout as you went in and the funny little vestibule at the back. There were about three dressing rooms, with two of them under the stage – you couldn't get away with that nowadays!

> I was involved with the first pantomime in the new theatre following the re-opening, 'Sleeping Beauty', and also helped start the Junior Arts Festival which first performed at the Winter Gardens and the Knightstone Theatre, but then moved to The Playhouse. I was involved with the Junior Arts Festival for about 30 years before it ended – when it started, it was only three days long and we built it up to seven days, becoming a member of All England, and therefore attracting talent from all over the country including London, Plymouth and Jersey.

'Barnum' production, 1994.
Photographs courtesy of Paddy Payne.

Over the years, Paddy created her own shows, including 'The Magic Minstrel Show', which then became 'Sunday Night Live' and attracted local celebrities to help her raise money:

> I ran 'Sunday Night Live' until 2014, and for three years Alex Beresford, the TV weatherman, compered the show for us. We also had radio presenters compere for us. We were very lucky. We raised money for the orthopaedic department at the hospital, as I had a connection to it, and we also raised money for Help for Heroes.

With her own dance school, Paddy supplied dancers and choreography for many performers over the years, including Stan Boardman and Tom O'Connor, as well as her own shows:

> I put on 'Barnum' at the theatre, which was fun. We had a tightrope put up, had aerial swinging and also had performers performing outside the building before people came in, as well as in the foyer, including fire eaters, jugglers, stilt walkers and clowns. It was an amateur production, but professional singer Alexia Gardner performed with us, which was a boost. I used a lot of local children with talent in my productions and gave them opportunities to headline shows.

*

Some of the members of The Friends of The Playhouse have also shared some of their memories and stories with me.

Freda Johnson told me that she has been involved with The Playhouse ever since joining The Friends in 1998. Having held various positions on the committee, Freda expressed what the theatre means to her: 'It's important to me. It's also important to the town as people enjoy coming to shows including people from all over. I've had a lot of fun and it's given me a lot of pleasure.'

Freda also recalled people she's met over the years:

> I've met a lot of people during my time at the theatre. Ken Dodd would

always give me a raffle prize when we did a Friends' raffle. I also talked with Jim Davidson before his show and he picked me out in the audience when he performed.

Andrew Gibson recollected a show which stands out in his memory, but not for the reason you might think:

> I remember seeing a show starring Brian Rix and there was a hailstorm outside. The noise became so much on the tin roof that in the end they had to stop and wait for it to quieten down before they could continue. Brian ended up sitting on the front edge of the stage with his feet dangling down while we waited!

*

An usherette who worked at the theatre in the 1980s recollected leaving the theatre following her shift, and being mistaken as part of a band.

> When I finished a shift, along with my friend, we went backstage to meet up with the band who had performed, The Dooleys. When they left the theatre by the stage door, there was a crowd of fans waiting to meet them and asking for autographs, and as me and my friend were with them, they asked for ours as well! So somewhere there are fans of The Dooleys with the autographs of usherettes!

*

A potentially worrying event in the late 1990s has stayed in Box Office Manager Julia Magor's memory, although it turned out to be quite a funny story. She told me:

> We received a call regarding the fire alarm in the middle of a sunny Sunday afternoon when the theatre was closed. On the way to the theatre we were expecting the worst, only to find when we got there the firemen were strolling round the outside of the building very unconcerned. It was discovered that a tour bus for a show the following day had parked up at the back of the theatre, and as it was a lovely sunny afternoon had decided to have a barbeque! The smoke from it had entered the theatre air vents and activated

the basement fire alarm. Thankfully all was well and we were given a tour of the bus, which was quite luxurious.

*

Pete Tilke shared with me a funny story that happened to fellow technician Dave Clothier during a show, which could have caused embarrassment to a performer:

> I do recollect a story that Dave shared with me. He told me that during a show he was flying the scenery and it was a big musical. There was one scene which was basically a black cloth far up stage, and at half stage there was a cloth with arches in it which went all across the stage. At the bottom of each arch there was a conduit which was there just to weigh the cloth down, so wherever the pillar was, there would be an arch, and that was the set on stage. Girls were dancing on the stage and the cue for the girls finishing the dance would be them with their hands up in the air. The plan was for the lights to go up in full, then there would be a blackout and the girls would come running off into the wings, and during the blackout, the arch cloth would be flown out and the stage set up for the next scene.
>
> The rehearsal went well, and on the first night, he was waiting in the wings and on standby for the cue. The girls were dancing and the number finished, the lights went to full, then they went to blackout, as planned. He was given the nod to fly the archways out, then flew the next cloth in, the lights came up on stage and, as they did, he was aware that one of the dancers was running down the wings with just her underwear and no costume on. Thinking he didn't remember it being in rehearsals, he then looked up and saw something on the bottom of the conduit and realised it was the girl's costume! It turns out he couldn't have timed it better, as when the stage went to blackout and the girls all put their hands up in the air, he flew the cloth out, and the conduit caught the bottom of her dress whipping her costume right off!

Dave also remembered this, telling me: 'You couldn't have rehearsed that happening. I was so embarrassed for her and couldn't stop apologising.'

*

Mark Thompson shared with me a few funny moments he can recall (although some names weren't disclosed), as well as some surreal moments for him personally:

> Ultimately performers are very normal – they are just like you and me. You can become quite complacent doing what I do and liaising with some performers, day in, day out, but there have been things which have made me smile over the years. We had a very high-profile comedian here once whose dog mounted me – there was some humour in that. There was also a high-profile '60s star who received a love letter here from a lady in the audience, saying that they had met each other in the '60s and had 'had a moment together', but he didn't remember it at all!

Mark told me that it tends to be the older performers who have an impact on him:

> The Stylistics were a big thing for me personally. They had never played Weston and it took me two years to actually get their promoter to come here. They were people I had grown up listening to, and sitting in the room with them was amazing. Sitting with Des O'Connor in his dressing room was surreal for me, as I remember thinking that I used to watch him on TV as a child. You hear about this 'diva' behaviour of some performers and there have been a few people I have had to be more direct with, but ultimately everyone is passionate about the theatre.

Ken Dodd is also up there in Mark's personal memories. Mark told me:

> The first time I was caught off guard to a certain extent was when Ken Dodd was here as he was just such a massive individual in the development of the arts, the theatre and the live experience. The first time I met him I sat in his dressing room with him. I had popped in to say 'hi' and to ask if everything was ok, and I was in there for about an hour and a half, as he told me some stories. That's what's different about that standard of performer – no one gave it to them, there was no quick route to success. Now there's 'X Factor' and 'Britain's Got Talent', which is a quick way to stardom, but people like Ken Dodd didn't have that and had to work for it. That's what was fascinating about meeting with him.

*

On a personal note, my first memory of performing at the theatre was when I was about nine years old, in a local dance festival called Dance Fest, with participants from many local dance schools. I remember thinking at the time 'I've made it', as I was going to perform in a real theatre and get ready in a professional dressing room.

The dressing room we used was situated below the stage and, from memory, we were told the trapdoor was right above us, so not only were we nervous about dancing on the stage, we also had the fear that the trapdoor could open and another dancer could fall on top of us! Having toured the theatre since, the trapdoor would not have been above our dressing room, but who were we to question it at the time? Maybe the fear of someone falling down on us was a way to get us to behave!

I remember having to wear bright blue eye shadow right up to our eyebrows, and bright red lipstick to make sure it could be seen by the audience under the lights – I can tell you I wasn't a fan of being 'plastered' with make-up and I remember thinking I didn't want to look like a clown. But when I saw that we all looked the same, I thought 'at least we all look silly and it's not just me!'

My family were in the audience as I performed and my mum had told me that she would wave at me so I could see where they were sitting, but with the bright lights shining, I could only see the front row of people, while the rest of the audience were in the dark. I remember feeling like a true performer.

Following my 'debut' performance at the theatre, it was another 20 years (giving away my age!) until I took to the stage again, this time in The Friends' pantomime in 2017. As much as I remembered enjoying being on the stage, I have to say that doing it when you're much older doesn't help with the nerves, but we all pulled together and managed to pull off a good performance. I must have enjoyed it, as I did it again in the summer of 2018, but while I do enjoy occasionally performing on stage, I find I'm more comfortable sitting in the audience.

Ghost Stories

Now, no theatre is complete without a ghost story, whether it's made up or true, and The Playhouse is no exception. While nothing has been proved (or should that be disproved?), there are a few rumours which have been shared over the years about the theatre.

I'd heard a rumour that someone had died falling from the roof of the theatre and questioned whether this had started the stories of ghosts, but Pete Magor set me straight: 'When the original theatre was modified and a hessian roof was added, there was a rumour that a man was doing maintenance on top of it and slipped down the hessian. It didn't kill him, but he was traumatised and subsequently died, so there's supposedly a ghost in the theatre connected with that.'

Pete also told me what he's been told, as well as some goings on which could be attributed to the supernatural: 'We've had mediums who have said there's a presence, as well as a lady ghost, but nothing has been proved, yet. I've been in the building on my own and I've heard doors go, as well as being in the basement and hearing things, but I've looked about and not seen anything.'

James Gentle, who works as an usher at the theatre, told me about his experiences when I asked him if he had seen a ghost:

> I think I have. I was walking through a door when completing my checklist at the end of the night and I thought I saw a figure up in the circle, something definitely moved. The lights were off and I was on my own. It was just me and the Front-of-House Manager in the building, and he was in his office; everyone else had gone home. I couldn't tell whether it was male or female, it was just a figure.

Dave Gentle, James's dad, is also convinced he's seen something:

> A personal experience I remember until this day was in the late '80s when I was leaving the theatre after finishing work and realised I'd forgotten my keys, so I went backstage to get them. Only the emergency lights were on, but they were enough to get around with. When I was on my way out of the green room, a figure appeared at the window in the doors which lead to the

corridor alongside the side of the stage, for about five seconds before moving on, which made me stop. I couldn't make out a face and assumed it was the manager, but when I eventually left, I discovered I'd been the only person in the building.

Dave also shared his sister's experiences with me:

My sister told me that in the mid '80s there was a singing group appearing at the theatre and one of the performers had a particular way of leaving her jewellery in her dressing room. Each night the dressing rooms were locked by the performers themselves, and only staff members of the theatre had another key. One morning when the lady entered her dressing room, her jewellery was all messed up and out of place. Thinking it was a prank, she laughed it off, but it kept happening night after night to the point where she had an uneasy feeling. All the staff promised it wasn't them, so imaginations ran wild. In the end she said, into the room, 'Leave me alone' and after that her jewellery remained where she left it.

It's up to you what you think about that story, could it have been a prank by a member of staff?

She also 'saw' something herself while working at the theatre. Part of the role of an usher/usherette is cleaning the auditorium after a performance, so after a show, my sister and her friend were in the circle, cleaning and chatting away, when a seat slowly went down as if someone was pulling it down to sit on it. There was no one else around and definitely no one else in the auditorium. Intrigued, they went to the seat [whose exact location and number will remain confidential to protect its identity!] to have a look, but by the time they got to it, it had already returned to its usual upright position.

Now if someone said that a seat went up by itself then you could attribute that to it getting stuck after being sat on and loosening, but how can you explain it going down by itself?

Footsteps have regularly been heard backstage when no one else seems to be around, but as Pete Tilke believes, this could have an innocent explanation:

Personally I've never experienced a ghost of any form, but I wouldn't rule it out. I think buildings have spirits and souls and I think when you are part of something you create an aura and that place changes as the people who use it change and move on. People have an affinity to a place and when you go somewhere you create a memory. I think the type of building that it is, there are a lot of energies and spirit feelings in it.

While Pete doesn't have any personal experiences of things which can't be explained, he did share with me a time when he was told of something in the immediate aftermath of it supposedly happening:

I can remember doing a show and the company crew only had about four men in it. We had completed the 'get-in', and one of the men, who I can only describe as a biggish 'biker' type of man, came to me with the Company Manager to ask whether it was possible to get from backstage to front of house without going through the auditorium. Unfortunately, that's not possible without being seen, so I explained ways they could go, and they told me they would go and explore, and off they went. About 45 minutes later, the Company Manager came back to me and said that they had gone the way I'd told them, but they had to turn back, as when they got to a door, the other man had opened it, jumped about two feet off the ground and fell back onto him, as he said some lady dressed in white had just scared the living daylights out of him. The Company Manager opened the door after him, but found nothing there. When I asked where the other man was, he told me he was in the bar having a whisky to calm his nerves as he was scared witless!

Another backstage member of staff has told about hearing doors open and close with no one else around, as well as of having a conversation with someone while making a set on stage and when referring to that conversation later on, being told that the other person wasn't there at the time.

Mark Thompson confirmed he has heard the rumours, but hasn't experienced anything himself and came up with a plausible explanation for the reported sightings:

I'm usually the last one here if there are no shows on and have walked through both the auditorium and basement without someone stopping me to say hello. I don't know how far it has gone with Chinese whispers, but the buildings on either side of the theatre are aware of the rumours and we all supposedly share an individual who has been 'seen'. There have been various sightings, but it's my understanding that they have all been very similar.

One explanation for the shared sightings of the individual who has been described as a lady dressed in white asking for help could be the lady who was murdered in 1844 near to where The Playhouse now stands. She was attacked in bed by her husband with a knife and killed. He appeared at the Somerset Assizes in Wells on 12th August 1844, where he was given the death sentence and consequently hanged in Taunton.

But, as Mark concluded after talking about the rumours: 'It's a big building with a lot of dark corners, so I can't confirm or deny, but I can say that theatres are small, close-knit communities where everyone knows everyone and everyone talks.'

So, while nothing has been proved or disproved when it comes to ghosts at the theatre, everyone has their own opinions, and who is anyone to question them? But rumours are a fact of life, and one thing's for sure, no amount of rumours will stop the public continuing to attend and enjoy the entertainment The Playhouse has to offer.

Brighter Prospects: 2000 to the Present Day

At the start of the new millennium, the future of The Playhouse Theatre looked bright, with audience numbers on the rise and support coming in thick and fast for the town's premier theatre. Support from The Friends of The Playhouse, who would soon celebrate their 10th anniversary, was also noted when it was reported at their annual general meeting that the previous year had been very successful indeed. Chairman John Ball praised the group on achieving a membership of 873, and Treasurer Brian Bell reported a very satisfactory balance in the accounts, noting that The Friends had contributed in excess of £46,000 to the theatre since their formation in 1991. Praising their fundraising efforts over the years, Front-of-House Manager Andy Jeffery said: 'The Friends of The Playhouse continue to support the theatre in a variety of ways for which the management and theatre staff are immensely grateful. Their contribution has enabled the theatre to deliver an even higher level of service.'

Money raised by The Friends was put into action when the theatre closed its doors in early June 2000 to allow £25,000 of improvements to take place, which encompassed: the expansion and upgrade of toilet facilities, including the creation of a disabled toilet; installation of a new lighting control panel which would enable Technical Manager Pete Magor to provide additional lighting effects for shows; an £800 gauze curtain being fitted to the stage; and 20 new sets of headphones bought for the hearing loop. The box office was also revamped with a change to the layout, and backstage staff also faced the task of replacing more than 200 sound and lighting dimmers as electricity was changed from analogue to digital. While these improvements took place, shows continued to take place, but were moved to the Winter Gardens, and the theatre re-opened in July with a screening of the Cary Grant film 'Arsenic and Old Lace'.

*

Having achieved success with 'Snow White and the Seven Dwarfs' at the start of 2000, once the theatre's doors re-opened The Playhouse continued to thrive, celebrating its most successful summer season in three years with box office figures showing an increase of £33,000 on the previous highest year of 1997. Despite the doors being closed for a month in order to carry out improvements over 20,000 people attended throughout the summer, with Jethro pulling in over 5,500 people during his residency at the theatre in July – even putting on an extra show to accommodate his fans – and Ken Dodd also playing his part when he performed two sold-out shows. Top names being talked about for the autumn season included comedienne Jo Brand, and sales for the upcoming pantomime 'Cinderella' starring household names Adele Silva (Kelly Windsor in 'Emmerdale') and Jack Douglas ('Carry On' films) were already 25% up on the previous year's figures. Andy Jeffery was understandably delighted at this and said: 'Comments from holiday-makers and local people alike have been excellent and our staff believe this success is due to a combination of several factors. One of the major influences on the rise in ticket sales is the nationally renowned stars and the high quality of the shows.'

The theatre's continuing success was confirmed when the autumn season reported higher audience figures than the previous year, and also proved to be the most successful autumn season in over five years. Sell-out shows from Barbara Dickson, Jo Brand and singer Charlie Landsborough contributed to this success, and during panto season, 'Cinderella' was bringing in the crowds, with sales up 52% on the previous year at the start of December. Andy Jeffery couldn't wait to share his praise for locals when he told the *Weston Mercury*:

> We have aimed to keep our shows affordable and enjoyable which I think reflects in the figures. The figures are especially impressive considering we have had less performances this year than previous years; it shows the theatre has earned a reputation with both performers and audiences as a provider of high-quality entertainment. Our loyal audience comes back time and time again and it is great to see the same friendly faces every season.

With 'Cinderella' set to be the most successful pantomime in the history of the theatre, it was reported that support was high, as people who had already seen the show were booking to see it for a second and even third time! Andy Jeffery was thrilled with this news, and shared his praise, saying:

> Weston is a small town and good news spreads fast. Word of mouth has served us well this year. Serious worries were considered when nearby theatres announced their panto line-up, but we are doing extremely well and that is all down to the actors, the quality of the venue and especially the loyal residents of Weston who continue to heap support on this important staple of the community.

At the beginning of 2001, it was confirmed that the year 2000 had cemented its place in the history of The Playhouse, when it was reported that the previous 12-month period had been the best in the 30-year history of the modern theatre. Smashing all previous box office records, both the summer and autumn seasons had hosted a variety of sell-out shows, and the year had been book-ended by two outstanding pantomimes, with both 'Snow White' and 'Cinderella' proving a success. A spokesman for The Playhouse told the *Weston Mercury*: 'During 2000 we staged 27 fewer shows than in 1999, but attendance and box office takings are well up on past seasons. Gross box office figures are around 12% up on the average figure for the previous four years.'

With the theatre receiving praise, tributes were also paid to theatre staff when both Andy Jeffery and Pete Magor were commended in leading showbiz magazine *Encore*. Andy was praised for his courtesy to promoters, putting him among the top theatre bosses in the country, and Pete Magor was voted 'Top Gaffer'.

*

Continuing to ride the wave of success over the next few years, with a line-up including old favourites such as Jethro and Ken Dodd as well as Bobby Davro, Bradley Walsh, Georgie Fame and Derek Acorah gracing the stage throughout the summer of 2002 it was reported in 2003 that, although the council was still subsidising the theatre at a cost of £320,000 per year, there was evidence that it was becoming more widely supported, with 52% of customers the previous year coming from outside Weston. Andy Jeffery, now Programming and Marketing Manager at the theatre, commented on the continued success, saying:

> We are going for quality shows with a good reputation and charge a reasonable ticket price – that seems to be working. The Playhouse is a very busy theatre and we hold about 300 performances a year, so we aim to ensure we get the right mix of exciting new shows and all-time favourites. We have a lovely intimate theatre which Bob Monkhouse once described as 'the comedian's playground'.

Although the theatre was doing well and public support was high, rumours circulated that its future could be limited, as the council still had to support it financially. Thankfully, Councillor Elfan Ap Rees set the record straight when he revealed that, while the council continued to support the theatre, it was hoping to reduce the subsidy: 'While we doubt if it can ever be made self-sustaining because of the size of the building, it is our aim to make it as commercial as possible. I see no reason for closing the theatre in the foreseeable future.'

As the theatre was continuing to cement its reputation as the place to go for entertainment in Weston, in 2004 it hosted a six-day festival to raise money for the entertainment charity, The Grand Order of the Water Rats. Opening with 'The Ken Dodd Laughter Show', Norman Wisdom, The Beverley Sisters, Joe Pasquale and Roy Hudd all performed to appreciative audiences, but with all this success, could the theatre sustain this level of entertainment and praise?

*

In order to keep the theatre fresh and up to date, it was closed in the latter part of 2004 to allow a £100,000 refurbishment to take place – the biggest it had undergone in many years. Giving the theatre a complete facelift, all 664 seats, as well as the carpets, were replaced. While the seats had previously been re-upholstered, this was the first time they had been fully replaced since the theatre was re-opened in 1969! It was estimated that 3.5 million people had sat on those seats during this time, so it was fair to say it was time for replacements. Pete Magor recalled taking the seats out and how odd the theatre looked without them:

> It looked empty when there were no seats or carpets. There must have been about 12 of us taking the seats out – there was a group of lads who came to help us and at the time they were putting in seats in a stadium, so this was a small amount for them. One guy in the balcony had an idea and kicked the seats once they'd been loosened and they then concertinaed down – we filled so many skips with them all. People don't realise how worn the seats get. Every now and then when the theatre is closed seats will go away and get replaced, but this is done on an individual basis now rather than the whole lot at once.

The seats being taken out had their sponsorship plaques attached to them, but as the seats were being replaced and to save them getting lost, the plaques were removed and put on a board which is now on display in the bar area of the theatre.

Also included in the refurbishment was another change of layout in the box office, an upgrade of the disabled facilities, and the addition of a follow spot in the projection box at the back of the circle. With all the hard work and effort being put into giving the theatre a facelift, you would be forgiven for thinking it would have been closed for quite some time to allow all the work to be completed, but in fact the whole project took less than four weeks.

However, despite increased audience numbers and improvements made to the theatre, its future was under threat again when a leaked email sent to North Somerset Council was made public in September 2007. The Friends of The Playhouse were angry at the news that the theatre, for which they had raised £100,000 over the years, could be closed by the council in a bid to save money. The 750-member-strong group were determined to fight for the theatre and told the *Weston Mercury*: 'This has been an ongoing threat for four years and we will fight tooth and nail to keep it open.' Having already lost the Tropicana and the Knightstone, they felt that:

> To close the theatre would be a great blow to residents. People from around the country also visit the theatre which generates a vast amount of business

Seat sponsorship plaques now
displayed in the bar area.
Author's photograph.

for the town. The artistes are passionate about The Playhouse and consider
it one of the friendliest theatres in the country.

Deputy Leader of North Somerset Council Elfan Ap Rees spoke out in
response, saying 'The Playhouse is the responsibility of the Executive
Member for Community Services, but we are having to look at all activities
carried out by the council if we are to maintain a minimum council tax
increase.'

Thankfully, while cost savings needed to be made by the council, The
Playhouse remained untouched and was allowed to live on for another day.

*

With the threat of closure never far away, a change came in April 2011 when
Parkwood Leisure diversified into theatre management and took over the

running of the theatre, meaning that it would no longer be financially supported by the council. Winning a 10-year contract to run both The Playhouse and the Winter Gardens, Parkwood Leisure soon began to do things differently, but with their background in running leisure centres, not everyone was too happy with the changes. It was reported in the local press in 2013 that concerns had been raised over the running of the theatre, as in the two years since it had been taken over, all of the senior managers had either left through resignation, retirement or relocation or else had been made redundant. Other staff members had been required to take on extra duties, and the level of customer service had dropped, meaning that there were yet again threats to close the theatre. In response to the rumours, Parkwood Leisure spoke out against this, insisting that there were 'plans to invest into both venues to ensure they remain at the heart of Weston for years to come', which has been the case, although the ownership of the Winter Gardens was later, in 2015, transferred to Weston College.

Despite the concerns about how the theatre was being run, reports showed in early 2014 that sales at The Playhouse had gone up 6.7% in the past year, with the number of tickets sold totalling 90,350. Record sales were recorded for pantomime 'Jack & the Beanstalk' in 2013, and praise was given to Parkwood Leisure in its turnaround of the theatre. It was also announced that further staffing changes were to take place, with Andy Jeffery, General Manager, leaving his post, and Mark Thompson, whose theatre background was in educational theatre shows for children, set to replace him.

Having already had a successful run of comedy at the theatre, with Jason Manford, Jon Richardson and Josh Widdicombe all performing and with sales on the up, The Playhouse experienced a further huge outpouring of support, when tickets to see comedian Lee Evans in two performances in June 2014 all sold out in record time. Mark recalled: 'When we had Lee Evans we announced it locally and didn't put the tickets online, we just said that they would be available at the box office. I got here at 8.40 am and there was a queue as far back as the bank!'

Starting as he meant to go on, Mark led a revamp of the theatre during the summer of 2014 in partnership with Parkwood Leisure, North Somerset Council and The Friends of The Playhouse. A total of £47,000 was spent on giving both the front of the theatre and box office a facelift, including new lighting and décor in the box office, a new LED canopy to light up The Playhouse sign at the front of the theatre and two TV screens fitted outside to advertise future productions, and a new sound system was also installed in the auditorium. Realising the theatre had become a little tired, Mark was quoted in the local press as saying: 'Over the years the theatre has begun to look a little dated but with the changes we have made over the past few months, it's finally back to its former glory as the home of Weston entertainment.'

As well as upgrading the building itself, Mark had big ambitions for the theatre, and so 2015 was the start of bigger shows arriving at the venue. He told me 'The period of 2015-16 was when it was really exciting as I was managing to pull shows in that had never been here, and watching how Weston reacted to some of those shows was incredible.'

The first of these big shows was murder mystery play 'The Mousetrap', which ran at the theatre between 13th and 18th July 2015. More than 4,300 people saw the show during its eight performances, and the £100,000 mark was broken at the box office for the first time in the theatre's 69-year history. Mark recalls how people reacted when they learnt it wasn't a local production, saying: 'The number of people I would see coming to the box office asking if it was a local production and the way they reacted to it being the West End production was exciting.'

With the theatre receiving a certificate of excellence from TripAdvisor in the same month, The Playhouse was firmly on the map, and another West End show, 'Blood Brothers', starring Maureen Nolan, followed in October, quickly taking over as the highest-grossing production, selling 4,904 tickets during the week-long run. Being the biggest production the theatre had ever staged, it took six months for the venue to prepare for it, and road closures were arranged for its arrival due to the additional transport needed. Mark said at the time:

> It really is our biggest challenge to date and I'm sure many lessons will be learned over the coming week. The venue has been stripped back to the bare walls to ensure the set fits within our intimate environment and weeks of preparation have taken place to ensure a smooth transition. Hopefully this

will take us to the next stage and pave the way for more exciting announce-
ments in the future.

Taking a risk on such a big production certainly paid off, as 'Joseph and the
Technicolor Dreamcoat' appeared at the theatre less than 12 months later
and smashed box office records again when 5,500 seats were sold. It was
reported that box office takings had increased by 43% in the last two years,
and that more West End Shows would be appearing at the theatre, with Mark
saying: 'We're delighted with the attendance figures for "Joseph", which once
again further cements our town's home of entertainment as a place that we
can be proud of.' He added: 'Bringing the West End shows is really putting
us and Weston on the map, with more shows due to arrive this year, including "Footloose", "Avenue Q" and "Rehearsal for Murder".'

Audiences have since continued to be drawn to the theatre by bigger shows
including: the stage adaptation of 'The Shawshank Redemption' in September 2016, produced by West End legend Bill Kenwright; musical 'Save the
Last Dance for Me' starring Antony Costa from Blue; and David Walliams'
'Gangsta Granny' prior to its West End run in October. Musicals 'Dreamboats & Petticoats' and 'Our House', starring 'Britain's Got Talent' winner
George Sampson, provided plenty of smiles, and Maureen Nolan also made
a welcome return to the theatre starring in 'Menopause the Musical' in 2017.

*

While The Playhouse has continued a good run over the last few years, it
suffered a mishap in April 2017 when a severe flood in the backstage and
basement area of the theatre caused the show in progress to be cancelled,
and the theatre subsequently closed for three days. Thanks to the swift
actions of the theatre staff, the children taking part in the North Somerset
Dance Festival and all audience members were quickly but calmly escorted
out of the building, while the fire service attended to do what they could to
help prevent further damage. When I spoke to Pete Tilke about the incident,
he recalled:

We were about 15 minutes into the show when a teacher came up to me on
the side of the stage and said one of the hydrants had gone off backstage, so

I was thinking a fire extinguisher. But when I was walking along the corridor past dressing rooms 3 to 6, I could see water coming out a hole in the wall, and it was coming out at such force that it was actually pushing the emergency swing doors open, and I'm thinking, this doesn't look good and can I put anything in it to stop it? Basically I ran downstairs to see if I could isolate it and I couldn't, so ran on the stage and said to the compere that we need to stop the show. We brought the iron curtain down and we evacuated everybody, and all the training that we've done proved valuable as we got everyone out in a very good time.

Literally, the backstage area from the first floor to the basement was under two inches of water, so it had ruined dressing rooms 1 and 2, the carpets and flooring in the other dressing rooms, and all my lights that I store in the dimmer room were gone. It wasn't a great weekend. We knew we were going to cancel the next two days – the Friday and Saturday – and thankfully we didn't have a show on the Sunday, so we came in all four days just to clear up and clean it, to get the venue into a state where we could welcome the public and the artists back on stage.

Thankfully, there was no lasting damage to the theatre, and everyone involved was praised by Mark when he gave an interview to the local press, saying: 'All individuals from the performing schools and all audience members in the auditorium were evacuated safely and in a timely fashion. Our thanks to all of the audience members for their assistance, the support from the community and the fantastic service provided by the Weston Fire Brigade.'

Looking Ahead to the Future

Over the years it's fair to say The Playhouse Theatre has had its ups and downs, but it has continued to prove itself as the home of live entertainment in Weston and has kept going despite the odds stacking against it at times. With variety remaining at the heart of the theatre, week-long performances continue to mix with one-night shows, and the scope of performers continues to grow.

As more top entertainers, including Jimmy Carr, Sally Morgan, Russell Watson, Jimmy Osmond, Tim Vine, Henning Wehn and many more, add The Playhouse to their tour lists, the theatre continues to provide local talent, including amateur societies as well as local dance schools, with a place to perform and is continually growing its appeal to locals and holiday-makers as well as people travelling from further afield, having been tempted by what it has to offer.

With family shows, tribute acts, concerts, local talents, comedians, singers and dance shows provided throughout the year, the theatre really is the home of variety. So, while The Playhouse celebrates the 50-year anniversary of the re-opening following the fire which could have spelt the end of it, what does the future hold for the town's premier theatre which has refused to give in to destruction and frequent threats of closure over the years?

Mark Thompson told me:

> It's really about continuing to establish the theatre as a number one touring venue which shows want to come to, and that shift has happened. Promoters now approach the theatre rather than us chasing shows and I select what product goes into the venue – that's a really good change.

Celebration of the history of
The Playhouse.
Author's photograph.

A regional theatre has the ability to be the hub of a town, and I think there's still work to be done locally in regards to developing new audiences. At some point if space would allow, I would like to introduce some sort of theatre school to allow us to encourage home-grown talent. Something I think is apparent in our in-house productions over the past four years is that there's a lot of talented children in Weston, so it would be good to find new ways to engage with them. The theatre has come a long way. The growth has been phenomenal over the past four years, but by no means are we done.

*

With framed displays taking pride of place on the staircase in the bar area setting out the history of the theatre, the fire, the rebuild and the re-opening, The Playhouse is clearly justifiably proud of its history.

It'll be exciting to see what the future holds for The Playhouse – so here's to the next 50 years.

Index of Shows

Index

Acknowledgements and Thank-yous

Sue Ball – who supported me, read through everything I wrote and also typed my research notes; Julia Magor; Pete Magor; Tony Blizzard; Mark Thompson; Vicki Gray; Dave Gentle, James Gentle; Brian Austin; The Friends of The Playhouse; Pete Tilke; Andrew and Lorna Gibson (information and pictures); Neil Gibson (pictures); David Driver; *Weston Mercury* (pictures); Sir Ken Dodd OBE; Somerset Heritage Centre; Anthony Keyes; Wendy Summers; Freda Johnson; Ian Gibson and family; Karolina McIntyre; Paddy Payne, Rosemary Dowie; Pauline Preistman; David Andrews (information & pictures); Weston Library local history room; V&A Archives, London; Edna and Aubrey Neale; Dave Clothier; Sharon Poole (photos); Grove House (photo of The Playhouse token key); Weston Operatic Society (photos); Tony Lay, President of Worle Operatic and Dramatic Society; Russell Scott, Worle Operatic and Dramatic Society; Mike and Trish Kemp; John and Rachel Wiltshire; Ken Coles, President of Weston Operatic Society.

Bibliography/Sources of Information

BBC News website, 19th May 2003
http://news.bbc.co.uk/1/hi/england/somerset/3040115.stm
Bristol Evening Post (1964-2004)
David Jason: *My Life* (Random House 2013)
Bob Monkhouse: *Crying with Laughter: My Life Story* (Arrow Books 1993)
Brian Rix: *Tour De Farce A Tale of Touring Theatres and Strolling Players (from Thespis to Branagh)* (Hodder & Stoughton 1992)
Western Daily Press (1965-1968)
Weston Mercury & Somersetshire Herald (now known as the *Weston Mercury*) newspaper on microfilm (1948-1999)
Weston & Worle News (1992-1999)
www.somersetlive.co.uk – article 5th October 2017